cook's library

Quick
& Easy

cook's library

Quick
& Easy

p

This is a Parragon Publishing Book
This edition published in 2004

Parragon Publishing
Queen Street House
4 Queen Street
Bath BA1 1HE, UK

ISBN: 0-75259-954-2

Printed in China

NOTE

Cup measurements in this book are for American cups. This book
uses imperial and metric measurements. Follow the same units of
measurement throughout; do not mix imperial and metric. All spoon
measurements are level: teaspoons are assumed to be 5 ml,
and tablespoons are assumed to be 15 ml. Unless otherwise stated,
milk is assumed to be full fat, eggs and individual vegetables such
as potatoes are medium, and pepper is freshly ground black pepper.

The times given for each recipe are an approximate guide only because
the preparation times may differ according to the techniques used by
different people and the cooking times may vary as a result of the type
of oven used. The preparation times include chilling and marinating
times, where appropriate.

Recipes using raw or very lightly cooked eggs should be avoided
by infants, the elderly, pregnant women, convalescents, and anyone
suffering from an illness.

Contents

Introduction

This book is designed to appeal to anyone who wants a wholesome but quick and easy diet, and includes many recipes suitable for vegetarians and vegans. Its main aim is to show people that, with a little forethought, it is possible to spend very little time in the kitchen while still enjoying appetizing food.

The recipes collected together come from all over the world; some of the Asian and barbecue dishes featured require marinating, often overnight, but it is worth remembering that their actual cooking time is very short once the marinade has been absorbed.

The more exotic dishes on offer are balanced by some traditional dishes, which are sure to become firm family favorites. If you want fast food for everyday meals, or you are short on time and want to prepare a tasty dinner party treat, there is something for everybody in this book. To save time in the kitchen, always make sure you have a stock of staple foodstuffs such as rice, pasta, spices, and herbs, so you can easily turn your hand to any number of these recipes.

Ingredients

Grains and Rice

A good variety of grains is essential. For rice, choose from long-grain, basmati, risotto, short-grain, and wild rice. Look out for fragrant Thai rice, jasmine rice, and combinations of different varieties to add color and texture to your dishes. When choosing your rice, remember that brown rice is a better source of vitamin B_1 and fiber. Other grains add variety to the diet. Try to include some barley, millet, bulgar wheat, polenta, oats, semolina, sago, and tapioca.

Pasta

Pasta is very popular nowadays, and there are many types and shapes to choose from. Keep a good selection, such as basic lasagna sheets, tagliatelle or fettuccine, and spaghetti. For a change, sample some of the many fresh pastas now available. Better still, make your own—handrolling pasta can be very satisfying, and you can buy a special machine for rolling the dough and cutting certain shapes.

Noodles

The Chinese use several varieties of noodle. You will probably find it easier to use the readily available dried varieties, such as egg noodles, which are yellow, rice stick noodles, which are white, and very fine, or transparent noodles, which are opaque when dry and turn transparent on cooking. However, cellophane or rice noodles may be used instead.

Beans

Beans are a valuable source of protein, vitamins, and minerals. Stock up on soybeans, Great Northern beans, red kidney beans, cannellini beans, garbanzo beans, lentils, and wax beans. Buy dried beans for soaking and cooking yourself, or canned varieties for speed and convenience.

Bean Curd

This soybean paste is available in several forms. The cake variety, which is soft, spongy and a white-gray color, is used in this book. It is bland, but adds texture and is perfect for absorbing all the other flavors in the dish.

Herbs

A good selection of herbs is important for adding variety to your cooking. Fresh herbs are preferable to dried, but it is essential to have dried ones as a back-up. You should store dried thyme, bay leaves, oregano, rosemary, mixed herbs, and bouquet garni envelopes.

Chinese Five-Spice Powder

An aromatic blend of cinnamon, cloves, star anise, fennel, and brown peppercorns. It is often used in marinades.

Szechuan Pepper

This is quite hot and spicy, and should be used sparingly. It is red in color and is available from supermarkets, and specialist Asian grocery stores.

Star Anise

This is an eight-pointed, star-shaped pod with a strong aniseed flavor. The spice is also available ground. If a pod is added to a dish, it should be removed before serving.

Chiles

These come both fresh and dried and in many varieties. The "hotness" varies so use with caution. The "heat" is contained in the seeds and membrane, which are often discarded. Chili powder should always be used sparingly. Check whether the powder is pure chili or a chili seasoning or blend, which should be milder.

Nuts and Seeds

As well as adding protein, vitamins and useful fats to the diet, nuts and seeds add important flavor and texture to vegetarian meals. Make sure you keep a good supply of nuts, such as hazelnuts, pine nuts, and walnuts. Coconut is useful too. For your seed collection, have sesame, sunflower, and poppy. Pumpkin seeds, in particular, are a good source of zinc.

Bok Choy

Also known as pak choi or Chinese cabbage, this has a mild, slightly bitter flavor.

Bamboo Shoots

These are added for texture, as they have little flavor. Available in cans, they are a common ingredient in Chinese cooking.

Bean Sprouts

These are mung bean shoots, which are nutritious and contain many vitamins. They add crunch to a recipe. Do not overcook them, or they will wilt.

Dried Fruits

Currants, raisins, golden raisins, dates, apples, apricots, figs, pears, peaches, prunes, papayas, mangoes, figs, bananas, and pineapples can all be purchased dried and can be used in lots of different recipes. When buying dried fruits, look for untreated varieties: for example, buy figs that have not been rolled in sugar, and choose unsulphured apricots, if they are available.

Oils and Fats

Oils are useful for adding subtle flavorings to foods, so it is a good idea to have a selection in your pantry. Use a light olive oil for cooking and extra virgin olive oil for salad dressings. Use corn oil as a good all-purpose oil. Sesame oil is wonderful in stir-fries; hazelnut and walnut oils are superb in salad dressings. Oils and fats add flavor to foods, and contain the important fat-soluble vitamins A, D, E, and K. Remember that all fats and oils are high in calories, and that oils are higher in calories than butter.

Sesame Oil

This is made from roasted sesame seeds and has an intense flavor. It burns easily and is added at the end of cooking for flavor, and is not used for cooking.

Chinese Rice Wine

This is very similar to dry sherry in color, alcohol content, and smell. It is worth buying Chinese rice wine for its distinctive flavor.

Vinegars

Choose three or four vinegars—red or white wine, hard cider, light malt, sherry, or balsamic vinegar, to name just a few. Each adds its own character to your recipes.

Rice Vinegar

This has a mild, sweet taste that is quite delicate. It is available in some supermarkets, but if it is not available use hard cider vinegar instead.

Mustards

Mustards are made from black, brown, or white mustard seeds, which are ground and mixed with spices. Meaux mustard is made from mixed mustard seeds and has a grainy texture with a warm taste. Dijon mustard, made from husked and ground mustard seeds, has a sharp flavor. Its versatility in salads and with barbecues makes it ideal for vegetarians. German mustard is mild and is best used in Scandinavian and German dishes, and American mustard is also mild and quite sweet. English mustard is quite hot and is used with beef and ham.

Sauces

Teriyaki sauce gives an authentic Japanese flavor to stir-fries. Black bean and yellow bean sauces add an instant authentic Chinese flavor to stir-fries.

Soy Sauce

This is widely available from supermarkets and Asian grocery stores, but it is worth buying a good grade. It is produced in both light and dark varieties—the former is used with fish and vegetables for a lighter color and flavor, while the latter, being richer, saltier, and more intense, is used as a dipping sauce or with strongly flavored meats.

Using Spices

You can use spices whole, ground, roasted, fried, or mixed with yogurt to marinate meat and poultry. One spice can alter the flavor of a dish and a combination of several can produce different colors and textures. The quantities of spices shown in the recipes are merely a guide. Increase or decrease them as you wish, especially in the cases of salt and chili powder, which are a matter of taste. Many of the recipes in this book call for ground spices, which are generally available in supermarkets as well as in specialist Asian grocery stores. In India whole spices are ground at home, and there is no doubt that freshly ground spices do make a noticeable difference to the taste.

Some recipes require roasted spices. In India, this is done on a *thawa*, but you can use a heavy, ideally cast-iron skillet. No water or oil is needed: the spices are simply dry-roasted whole while the skillet is shaken to stop them burning on the bottom of the skillet.

Remember that long cooking over a low heat will improve the taste of the food as it lets the spices be absorbed. This is why reheating dishes the following day is no problem for most Asian food.

Basic Recipes

These recipes form the basis of several of the dishes contained throughout this book. Many of these basic recipes can be made in advance and stored for 2 days in the refrigerator or until required.

Basic Tomato Sauce

2 tbsp olive oil

1 small onion, chopped

1 garlic clove, chopped

14 oz/400 g canned chopped tomatoes

2 tbsp chopped fresh parsley

1 tsp dried oregano

2 bay leaves

2 tbsp tomato paste

1 tsp sugar

salt and pepper

1 Heat the olive oil in a skillets over a medium heat. Add the onion and cook for 2–3 minutes, or until translucent. Add the garlic and cook for 1 minute.

2 Stir in the tomatoes with their juice, parsley, oregano, bay leaves, tomato paste, and sugar. Season to taste with salt and pepper.

3 Bring the sauce to a boil, then let simmer for 15–20 minutes, or until reduced by half. Taste the sauce and adjust the seasoning, if necessary. Discard the bay leaves just before serving.

Béchamel Sauce

1¼ cups milk

2 bay leaves

3 whole cloves

1 small onion

¼ cup butter

6 tbsp flour

1¼ cups light cream

large pinch of freshly grated nutmeg

salt and pepper

1 Pour the milk into a saucepan and add the bay leaves. Press the cloves into the onion, add to the pan and bring the milk to a boil over a low heat. Remove from the heat, cover and let cool.

2 Strain the milk into a jug and rinse out the pan, then melt the butter in the pan over a low heat. Stir in the flour for 1 minute, then gradually pour in the milk, stirring constantly. Cook for 3 minutes, then pour in the cream and bring to a boil. Remove from the heat and season to taste with nutmeg, salt, and pepper.

Cheese Sauce

2 tbsp butter

1 tbsp flour

1 cup + 2 tbsp milk

2 tbsp light cream

pinch of freshly grated nutmeg

½ cup grated sharp cheddar cheese

1 tbsp freshly grated Parmesan cheese

salt and pepper

1 Melt the butter in a saucepan over a low heat. Stir in the flour and cook for 1 minute. Gradually pour in the milk, stirring. Stir in the cream and season to taste with nutmeg, salt, and pepper.

2 Let simmer for 5 minutes, then remove from the heat and stir in the cheeses. Stir until the cheeses have melted and blended into the sauce, adjust the seasoning and serve or use as required.

Espagnole Sauce

2 tbsp butter

¼ cup all-purpose flour

1 tsp tomato paste

1 cup hot veal bouillon

1 tbsp Madeira

1½ tsp white wine vinegar

2 tbsp olive oil

2 strips bacon, diced

3 tbsp diced carrot

3 tbsp diced onion

3 tbsp diced celery

3 tbsp sliced leek

2 tbsp diced fennel

1 fresh thyme sprig

1 bay leaf

1 Melt the butter in a saucepan over a low heat. Add the flour and cook, stirring, until lightly colored. Add the tomato paste, then stir in the bouillon, Madeira, and white wine vinegar. Cook for 2 minutes.

2 Heat the oil in a separate saucepan over a medium heat. Add the bacon, carrot, onion, celery, leek, fennel, thyme, and bay leaf and cook until softened. Remove the vegetables from the pan with a slotted spoon and drain. Add the vegetables to the sauce and let simmer for 4 hours, stirring occasionally. Strain the sauce before using.

Ragu Sauce

3 tbsp olive oil

3 tbsp butter

2 large onions, chopped

4 celery stalks, sliced thinly

6 oz/175 g bacon, chopped

2 garlic cloves, chopped

1 lb/450 g ground lean beef

2 tbsp tomato paste

1 tbsp flour

14 oz/400 g canned chopped tomatoes

⅔ cup beef bouillon

⅔ cup red wine

2 tsp dried oregano

½ tsp freshly grated nutmeg

salt and pepper

1 Heat the oil and butter in a saucepan over a medium heat. Add the onions, celery and bacon and cook for 5 minutes, stirring.

2 Stir in the garlic and ground beef and cook, stirring until the meat has lost its redness. Reduce the heat and cook for 10 minutes, stirring constantly.

3 Increase the heat to medium, stir in the tomato paste and flour, then cook for 1–2 minutes. Stir in the tomatoes, bouillon, and wine and bring to a boil. Season to taste with salt and pepper and stir in the oregano and nutmeg. Cover and let simmer for 45 minutes. The sauce is now ready to use.

Italian Red Wine Sauce

⅝ cup beef bouillon

⅔ cup Espagnole Sauce (see left)

½ cup red wine

2 tbsp red wine vinegar

4 tbsp chopped shallots

1 bay leaf

1 fresh thyme sprig

pepper

1 Make a demiglace sauce. Mix the beef bouillon and Espagnole Sauce in a saucepan and heat for 10 minutes, stirring occasionally.

2 Meanwhile, place the red wine, red wine vinegar, shallots, bay leaf, and thyme in a saucepan, bring to a boil over a low heat and reduce by three-quarters.

3 Strain the demiglace sauce and add to the saucepan containing the red wine sauce and let simmer for 20 minutes, stirring occasionally. Season with pepper to taste and strain the sauce before using.

How to Use This Book

Each recipe contains a wealth of useful information, including a breakdown

of nutritional quantities, preparation, and cooking times, and level of difficulty.

All of this information is explained in detail below.

A full-color photograph
of the finished dish.

114

QUICK & EASY

Chicken pieces are cooked
in a succulent, mild
mustard and lemon sauce,
then coated in poppy seeds
and served on a bed of
fresh pasta shells.

Lemon Chicken Conchiglie

SERVES 4

8 chicken pieces, about 115 g/4 oz each
55 g/2 oz butter, melted
4 tbsp mild mustard (see Cook's Tip)
2 tbsp lemon juice
1 tbsp brown sugar
1 tsp paprika
3 tbsp poppy seeds
400 g/14 oz fresh pasta shells
1 tsp olive oil
salt and pepper

1. Arrange the chicken pieces, smooth-side down, in a single layer in a large ovenproof dish.

2. Mix the butter, mustard, lemon juice, sugar and paprika together in a bowl and season to taste with salt and pepper. Brush half the mixture over the upper surfaces of the chicken pieces and bake in a preheated oven at 200°C/400°F/ Gas Mark 6, for 15 minutes.

3. Remove the dish from the oven and carefully turn the chicken pieces over with tongs. Coat the upper surfaces of the chicken with the remaining mustard mixture, sprinkle the chicken pieces with poppy seeds and return to the oven for a further 15 minutes.

4. Meanwhile, bring a large saucepan of lightly salted water to the boil over a medium heat. Add the pasta shells and olive oil and cook for 8–10 minutes, or until tender, but still firm to the bite.

5. Drain the pasta thoroughly and arrange in a warmed serving dish. Top with the chicken, then pour over the sauce and serve immediately.

NUTRITION

Calories 652; Sugars 5 g; Protein 51 g;
Carbohydrate 46 g; Fat 31 g; Saturates 12 g

☆☆ easy
🕐 10 mins
🕐 35 mins

🍲 COOK'S TIP

Dijon is the type of mustard most often used in cooking, as it has a clean and only mildly spicy flavour. German mustard has a sweet-sour taste, with Bavarian mustard being slightly sweeter. American mustard is mild and sweet.

The ingredients for
each recipe are listed
in the order that they
are used.

The nutritional
information provided
for each recipe is per
serving or per portion.
Optional ingredients,
variations, or serving
suggestions have not
been included in the
calculations.

The method is clearly
explained with step-by-
step instructions that
are easy to follow.

Cook's tips provide useful
information regarding
ingredients or cooking
techniques.

⭐ The number of stars represents the difficulty of each recipe, ranging from very easy (1 star) to challenging (4 stars).

🕐 This amount of time represents the preparation of ingredients, including cooling, chilling, and soaking times.

🕐 This represents the cooking time.

Soups

A tasty soup that complements the dishes to follow can help set the tone for the rest of a meal, and the wide variety of dishes in this section offers a host of options to match almost any main course. The soups can also be light meals in themselves, served with fresh bread.

One of the great strengths of soups is their versatility. Although the best results are obtained from using fresh ingredients, soups are still a quick and easy way of using leftovers. Soup recipes can also be stretched to serve more people simply by increasing the amount of bouillon used. They can be thickened by adding more vegetables. If you have the time, making your own bouillon is a healthy alternative to using granules or bouillon cubes, which can contain salt and flavorings, and may have too strong a taste.

This soup is best made with white onions, which have a much milder flavor than the more usual brown variety. If these are unavailable, try using large Spanish onions instead.

Tuscan Onion Soup

SERVES 4

½ cup pancetta ham, diced
1 tbsp olive oil
4 large white onions, sliced thinly in rings
3 garlic cloves, chopped
3¾ cups hot chicken or ham bouillon
4 slices ciabatta or other Italian bread
3 tbsp butter
¾ cup coarsely grated Swiss or
    cheddar cheese
salt and pepper

1 Cook the pancetta in a large pan over a medium heat for 3–4 minutes, or until it starts to brown. Remove the pancetta from the pan and set aside until required.

2 Heat the olive oil in the pan over a high heat. Add the onions and garlic and cook for 4 minutes. Reduce the heat, cover and cook for 15 minutes, or until they are lightly caramelized.

3 Add the bouillon to the pan and bring to a boil over a medium heat. Reduce the heat and let simmer, covered, for about 10 minutes.

4 Toast the slices of ciabatta on both sides, under a preheated hot broiler, for 2–3 minutes, or until golden. Spread the ciabatta with the butter and top with the Swiss or cheddar cheese. Cut the bread into bite-size pieces.

5 Add the pancetta to the soup and season to taste with salt and pepper. Ladle to soup into 4 serving bowls and top with the toasted bread. Serve.

NUTRITION

Calories *390*; Sugars *0 g*; Protein *9g*;
Carbohydrate *15 g*; Fat *33 g*; Saturates *14 g*

⭐ very easy

🕐 5–10 mins

🕐 40–45 mins

 COOK'S TIP

Pancetta is similar to bacon, but it is air- and salt-cured for about 6 months. It is available from most delicatessens and some large supermarkets. If you cannot obtain pancetta, use unsmoked bacon instead.

This wonderful combination of cannellini beans, vegetables, and vermicelli is made even richer by the addition of pesto, dried mushrooms, and Parmesan cheese.

Vegetable *and* Bean Soup

1 Slice the eggplant into rings about ½-inch/1-cm thick, then cut each ring into 4 pieces.

2 Cut the tomatoes and potato into small dice. Cut the carrot into sticks, about 1-inch/2.5-cm long, and cut the leek into rings.

3 Place the cannellini beans and their liquid in a large pan. Add the eggplant, tomatoes, potatoes, carrot, and leek, stirring to mix.

4 Add the bouillon to the pan and bring to a boil over a medium heat. Reduce the heat and let simmer for 15 minutes.

5 Add the basil, dried mushrooms and their soaking liquid, and the vermicelli, then let simmer for 5 minutes, or until all the vegetables are tender. Remove the pan from the heat and stir in the pesto.

6 Ladle the soup into 4 warmed serving bowls and serve immediately with freshly grated Parmesan cheese, if you wish.

SERVES 4

1 small eggplant
2 large tomatoes
1 potato, peeled
1 carrot
1 leek
15 oz/425 g canned cannellini beans
3¾ cups hot vegetable or chicken bouillon
2 tsp dried basil
1 tbsp dried porcini mushrooms, soaked for 20 minutes in enough warm water to cover
¼ cup dried vermicelli
3 tbsp pesto (store bought)
freshly grated Parmesan cheese, to serve (optional)

NUTRITION
Calories *294*; Sugars *2 g*; Protein *11 g*;
Carbohydrate *30 g*; Fat *16 g*; Saturates *2 g*

⭐⭐   easy

    30 mins

    30 mins

A thick vegetable soup, which is a delicious meal in itself. Serve with Parmesan cheese and lots of warm sun-dried tomato bread.

Garbanzo Bean Soup

SERVES 4

2 tbsp olive oil
2 leeks, sliced
2 zucchini, diced
2 garlic cloves, minced
1 lb 2 oz/800 g canned chopped tomatoes
1 tbsp tomato paste
1 bay leaf
3¾ cups chicken bouillon
1½ cups canned garbanzo beans, drained and rinsed
8 oz/225 g fresh spinach
salt and pepper

to serve
freshly grated Parmesan cheese
sun-dried tomato bread

1 Heat the olive oil in a large pan over a medium heat. Add the leeks and zucchini and cook briskly for 5 minutes, stirring constantly.

2 Add the garlic, chopped tomatoes, tomato paste, bay leaf, chicken bouillon, and the garbanzo beans.

3 Bring to a boil and let simmer for 5 minutes.

4 Shred the spinach finely, add to the soup and cook for 2 minutes. Season to taste with salt and pepper.

5 Remove the bay leaf and discard. Ladle the soup into 4 warmed serving bowls and serve immediately with freshly grated Parmesan cheese and warm sun-dried tomato bread.

NUTRITION
Calories *297*; Sugars *0 g*; Protein *11 g*; Carbohydrate *24 g*; Fat *18 g*; Saturates *2 g*

 very easy
5 mins
15 mins

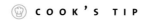 **COOK'S TIP**

Garbanzo beans are used extensively in North African cuisine and are also found in Spanish, Middle Eastern, and Asian cooking. They have a nutty flavor with a firm texture and are excellent canned.

The Calabrian mountains in southern Italy provide large amounts of exotic mushrooms. They are rich in flavor and color and make a wonderful soup.

Calabrian Mushroom Soup

1 Heat the olive oil in a large skillet over a low heat. Add the onion and cook for 3–4 minutes, or until softened and golden.

2 Wipe each mushroom with a damp cloth and cut any large mushrooms into smaller, bite-size pieces.

3 Add the mushrooms to the skillet, stirring quickly to coat them in the oil.

4 Add the milk to the skillet, bring to a boil over a medium heat, cover and let simmer for about 5 minutes. Gradually stir in the hot vegetable bouillon.

5 Toast the bread on both sides, under a preheated medium-hot broiler, for about 2–3 minutes, or until golden.

6 Mix the butter and garlic together, then spoon generously over the toast.

7 Place the toast in the bottom of a large tureen or divide it among 4 warmed serving bowls and pour over the hot soup. Top with the grated Swiss cheese and serve immediately.

SERVES 4

2 tbsp olive oil
1 onion, chopped
1 lb/450 g mixed mushrooms, such as porcini, oyster, and white
1¼ cups milk
3¾ cups hot vegetable bouillon
8 slices of French stick
3 tbsp butter, melted
2 garlic cloves, minced
¾ cup finely grated Swiss cheese
salt and pepper

NUTRITION
Calories 452; Sugars 5 g; Protein 15 g; Carbohydrate 42 g; Fat 26 g; Saturates 12 g

 COOK'S TIP

Mushrooms absorb liquid, which can lessen the flavor and affect cooking properties. Wipe them with a damp cloth rather than rinsing them in water.

easy

5 mins

25–30 mins

Plum tomatoes are ideal for making soups and sauces, as they have denser, less watery flesh than round varieties.

Tomato *and* Pasta Soup

SERVES 4

4 tbsp sweet butter
1 large onion, chopped
2¹/₂ cups vegetable bouillon
2 lb/900 g Italian plum tomatoes, peeled and coarsely chopped
pinch of baking soda
2 cups dried fusilli
1 tbsp superfine sugar
⁵/₈ cup heavy cream
salt and pepper
fresh basil leaves, to garnish
deep-fried croutons, to serve

1 Melt the butter in a large pan over a low heat. Add the onion and cook for 3 minutes. Add 1¹/₄ cups of vegetable bouillon to the pan, with the chopped tomatoes and baking soda. Bring the soup to a boil, then let simmer for 20 minutes.

2 Remove the pan from the heat and let cool. Transfer the soup to a blender or food processor and process until a smooth purée forms. Pour through a fine strainer back into the rinsed-out pan.

3 Add the remaining vegetable bouillon and the pasta to the pan, and season to taste with salt and pepper.

4 Add the sugar to the pan and bring to a boil over a medium heat. Reduce the heat and let simmer for about 15 minutes.

5 Ladle the soup into 4 warmed serving bowls, swirl the cream on the top of the soup and garnish with fresh basil leaves. Serve with deep-fried croutons.

NUTRITION
Calories 503; Sugars 16 g; Protein 9 g;
Carbohydrate 59 g; Fat 28 g; Saturates 17 g

⭐⭐ easy
🕑 5 mins
🕐 50–55 mins

👨‍🍳 **COOK'S TIP**

To make orange and tomato soup, simply use half the quantity of vegetable bouillon, topped up with the same amount of fresh orange juice, and garnish the soup with orange peel.

This is a hearty and filling soup, as it contains rice and tender strips of lamb. Serve before a light main course.

Lamb *and* Rice Soup

1 Using a sharp knife, trim any fat from the lamb and discard. Cut the meat into thin strips and set aside until required.

2 Bring a large pan of lightly salted water to a boil over a medium heat. Add the rice, bring back to a boil, stir once, then reduce the heat and cook for 10–15 minutes, or until tender.

3 Drain the rice thoroughly, then rinse under cold running water, drain again and set aside until required.

4 Meanwhile, place the lamb bouillon in a large pan and bring to a boil over a medium heat.

5 Add the lamb strips, leek, garlic, soy sauce, and rice wine vinegar to the bouillon in the pan. Reduce the heat, cover, and let simmer for about 10 minutes, or until the lamb is tender and cooked through.

6 Add the mushroom slices and the rice to the pan and cook for an additional 2–3 minutes, or until the mushroom is cooked through. Ladle the soup into 4 warmed serving bowls and serve immediately.

SERVES 4

5½ oz/150 g lean lamb
¼ cup rice
3¾ cups lamb bouillon
1 leek, sliced
1 garlic clove, sliced thinly
2 tsp light soy sauce
1 tsp rice wine vinegar
1 medium open-cap mushroom, sliced thinly
salt

NUTRITION
Calories *116*; Sugars *0.2 g*; Protein *9 g*; Carbohydrate *12 g*; Fat *4 g*; Saturates *2 g*

easy

5 mins

35 mins

COOK'S TIP
Use a few dried Chinese mushrooms or porcini, rehydrated according to the package instructions and chopped, as an alternative to the open-cap mushroom. Add the Chinese mushrooms or porcini with the lamb in step 5.

Chinese mushrooms add an intense flavor to this soup, which is unique. Try to obtain them if you can, otherwise, use sliced open-cap mushrooms instead.

Chili Fish Soup

SERVES 4

1 tbsp dried Chinese mushrooms
2 tbsp corn oil
1 onion, sliced
1½ cups snow peas
3½ oz/100 g canned bamboo
   shoots, drained
3 tbsp sweet chili sauce
5 cups fish or vegetable bouillon
3 tbsp light soy sauce
2 tbsp fresh cilantro, plus extra
   to garnish (optional)
1 lb/450 g cod fillet, skinned and cubed

1 Place the mushrooms in a large bowl and pour over enough almost boiling water to cover. Let stand for 5 minutes, then drain the mushrooms thoroughly. Using a sharp knife, coarsely chop the mushrooms.

2 Heat the corn oil in a large preheated wok or large, heavy-bottomed pan over a medium heat. Add the onion and cook for 5 minutes, or until softened.

3 Add the snow peas, bamboo shoots, chili sauce, bouillon, and soy sauce and bring to a boil over a medium heat.

4 Reduce the heat, add the cilantro and cod, then let simmer for 5 minutes, or until the fish is cooked through.

5 Ladle the soup into 4 warmed serving bowls, garnish with extra cilantro, if you wish, and serve immediately.

NUTRITION

Calories 238; Sugars 1.4 g; Protein 21.4 g;
Carbohydrate 3.2 g; Fat 7.2 g; Saturates 1 g

 very easy

15 mins

15 mins

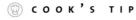 COOK'S TIP

There are many different varieties of dried mushrooms, but shiitake are best in this recipe. They are not cheap, but a small amount will go a long way.

Two classic ingredients in Chinese cooking, ginger and soy sauce, are blended together in this recipe for a very special soup. Light soy sauce is used as it will not overpower all the other flavors.

Crab *and* Ginger Soup

1 Place the carrot, leek, bay leaf, and fish bouillon into a large pan and bring to a boil over a medium heat. Reduce the heat, cover, and let simmer for about 10 minutes, or until the vegetables are nearly tender.

2 Meanwhile, remove the meat from the cooked crabs. Break off the claws, break the joints, and remove the meat (you may require a fork or skewer for this). Add the crabmeat to the fish bouillon in the pan.

3 Add the gingerroot, soy sauce, and star anise to the fish bouillon and bring to a boil over a medium heat. Reduce the heat and let simmer for about 10 minutes, or until all the vegetables are tender and the crab is heated through. Season to taste with salt and pepper.

4 Ladle the soup into 4 warmed serving bowls and serve immediately.

SERVES 4

1 carrot, chopped
1 leek, chopped
1 bay leaf
3¾ cups fish bouillon
2 medium-size cooked crabs
1-inch/2.5-cm piece fresh gingerroot, grated
1 tsp light soy sauce
½ tsp ground star anise
salt and pepper

NUTRITION
Calories 145; Sugars 2.4 g; Protein 40.9 g;
Carbohydrate 2.7 g; Fat 5.7 g; Saturates 2.6 g

 easy

 15 mins

15 mins

25 mins

👑 **COOK'S TIP**

If fresh crabmeat is unavailable, use drained canned crabmeat or thawed frozen crabmeat instead.

Tender cooked chicken strips and baby corn cobs are the main flavors in this delicious clear soup with just a hint of ginger.

Curried Chicken Soup

SERVES 4

1 cup canned corn, drained
3¾ cups chicken bouillon
12 oz/350 g cooked, lean chicken, cut into strips
16 baby corn cobs
1 tsp Chinese curry powder
½-inch/1-cm piece of fresh gingerroot, grated
3 tbsp light soy sauce
2 tbsp snipped fresh chives

NUTRITION
Calories *206*; Sugars *5 g*; Protein *29 g*; Carbohydrate *13 g*; Fat *5 g*; Saturates *1 g*

⭐⭐ easy

🕐 5 mins

🕐 30 mins

1 Place the canned corn in a food processor, with ⅔ cup of the chicken bouillon and process until a smooth purée forms.

2 Rub the corn purée through a fine strainer, pressing gently with the back of a spoon to separate the husks from the corn.

3 Pour the remaining chicken bouillon into a large pan and add the strips of cooked chicken. Stir in the corn purée and mix well.

4 Add the baby corn cobs and bring the soup to a boil over medium heat. Cook for 10 minutes.

5 Add the Chinese curry powder, grated gingerroot, and light soy sauce and stir well. Cook for an additional 10–15 minutes.

6 Stir in the snipped chives, then ladle the soup into 4 warmed serving bowls. Serve immediately.

 COOK'S TIP

Prepare the soup up to 24 hours in advance without adding the chicken. Let cool, cover, and store in the refrigerator. Add the chicken and heat the soup through thoroughly before serving.

This satisfying soup makes a good lunch or supper dish and you can use any vegetables that you have at hand. Children will love the tiny pasta shapes.

Chicken *and* Pasta Soup

1 Using a sharp knife, remove any skin from the chicken breasts and discard, then finely dice the chicken.

2 Heat the corn oil in a large pan over a medium heat. Add the chicken, onion, carrots, and cauliflower and quickly sauté until lightly colored.

3 Stir in the bouillon and herbs. Bring to a boil over a medium heat and add the pasta shapes. Return to a boil, cover, and let simmer for 10 minutes, stirring occasionally to prevent the pasta shapes sticking together.

4 Season to taste with salt and pepper. Ladle the soup into 4 warmed serving bowls and sprinkle with the Parmesan cheese, if you wish. Serve immediately with crusty bread.

SERVES 4

12 oz/350 g boneless chicken breasts
2 tbsp corn oil
1 medium onion, diced
1½ cups carrots, diced
2 cups cauliflower flowerets
3¾ cups chicken bouillon
2 tsp dried mixed herbs
1½ cups small dried pasta shapes
salt and pepper
freshly grated Parmesan cheese, for sprinkling (optional)
crusty bread, to serve

NUTRITION
Calories *185*; Sugars *5 g*; Protein *17 g*; Carbohydrate *20 g*; Fat *5 g*; Saturates *1 g*

easy

5 mins

15–20 mins

(🍴) **COOK'S TIP**

You can use any small pasta shapes for this soup—try conchigliette, ditalini, or even spaghetti broken up into small pieces. To make a fun soup for children, you could add animal-shaped or alphabet pasta.

This satisfying soup can be served as an entrée. You can add a mixture of rice and bell peppers to make it even more hearty, as well as colorful.

Chicken *and* Leek Soup

SERVES 4

2 tbsp butter

12 oz/350 g skinless, boneless chicken, cut into 1-inch/2.5-cm pieces

12 oz/350 g leeks, cut into 1-inch/ 2.5-cm pieces

5 cups chicken bouillon

1 bouquet garni envelope

8 pitted prunes

salt and white pepper

1 Melt the butter in a large heavy-bottomed pan over a medium heat. Add the chicken and leeks and cook for 8 minutes, stirring occasionally.

2 Add the chicken bouillon and bouquet garni envelope to the pan and stir well. Season to taste with salt and pepper.

3 Bring the soup to a boil over a medium heat, then reduce the heat and let simmer for 45 minutes.

4 Add the prunes to the pan and let simmer for 20 minutes. Remove the bouquet garni envelope and discard. Ladle the soup into 4 warmed serving bowls and serve.

NUTRITION
Calories *183*; Sugars *4 g*; Protein *21 g*; Carbohydrate *4 g*; Fat *9 g*; Saturates *5 g*

very easy

5 mins

1 hr 15 mins

COOK'S TIP

Instead of the bouquet garni envelope, you can use a bunch of fresh mixed herbs, tied together with string. Choose fresh herbs such as parsley, thyme, and rosemary.

Smoked haddock gives this soup a wonderfully rich flavor, while the mashed potatoes and cream thicken and enrich the bouillon.

Smoked Haddock Soup

1 Place the fish, onion, garlic, and water into a large, heavy-bottomed pan, then bring to a boil over a medium heat. Reduce the heat, cover, and let simmer for 15–20 minutes.

2 Remove the fish from the pan. Strip off the skin and remove all the bones, and set aside both. Flake the flesh finely with a fork.

3 Return the skin and bones to the cooking liquid and let simmer for about 10 minutes. Strain, discarding the skin and bones, then pour the cooking liquid into a clean pan.

4 Add the milk and flaked fish to the pan and season to taste with salt and pepper. Bring to a boil over a medium heat, then reduce the heat and let simmer for about 3 minutes.

5 Gradually whisk in sufficient mashed potato to give a fairly thick soup, then stir in the butter, and sharpen to taste with lemon juice.

6 Add the yogurt and 3 tablespoons of the chopped parsley. Reheat gently and adjust the seasoning, if necessary. Ladle the soup into 4 warmed serving bowls and sprinkle with the remaining parsley. Serve immediately.

SERVES 4

8 oz/225 g smoked haddock fillet
1 onion, chopped finely
1 garlic clove, minced
2½ cups water
2½ cups skim milk
2⅔–4 cups hot mashed potatoes
2 tbsp butter
about 1 tbsp lemon juice
6 tbsp lowfat plain yogurt
4 tbsp chopped fresh parsley
salt and pepper

NUTRITION
Calories *169*; Sugars *8 g*; Protein *16 g*;
Carbohydrate *16 g*; Fat *5 g*; Saturates *3 g*

easy

 25 mins

 40 mins

A mouthwatering, healthy vegetable, bean, and bacon soup. Serve it with plenty of granary or crusty whole-wheat bread.

Bacon, Bean, *and* Garlic Soup

SERVES 4

8 oz/225 g lean smoked back bacon slices
1 carrot, sliced thinly
1 celery stalk, sliced thinly
1 onion, chopped
1 tbsp oil
3 garlic cloves, sliced
3 cups hot vegetable bouillon
7 oz/200 g canned chopped tomatoes
1 tbsp chopped fresh thyme
14 oz /400 g canned cannellini beans,
    drained and rinsed
1 tbsp tomato paste
salt and pepper
freshly grated colby cheese, to garnish

1 Chop 2 slices of the bacon and place in a bowl. Cook in the microwave on High power for 3–4 minutes, until the fat runs out and the bacon is well cooked. Stir the bacon halfway through cooking to separate the pieces. Transfer the bacon to a plate lined with paper towels and let cool. When cool, the bacon pieces should be crisp and dry.

2 Place the carrot, celery, onion, and oil in a large bowl. Cover and cook on HIGH power for 4 minutes.

3 Chop the remaining bacon and add to the bowl with the garlic. Cover and cook on High power for 2 minutes.

4 Add the vegetable bouillon, chopped tomatoes, thyme, cannellini beans, and tomato paste. Cover and cook on High power for 8 minutes, stirring halfway through. Season to taste with salt and pepper. Ladle the soup into 4 warmed serving bowls and sprinkle with the crisp bacon and grated colby cheese. Serve immediately.

NUTRITION
Calories *261*; Sugars *5 g*; Protein *32 g*;
Carbohydrate *25 g*; Fat *8 g*; Saturates *2 g*

easy

5 mins

20 mins

COOK'S TIP

For a more substantial soup add ¹/₂ cup small dried pasta shapes or short lengths of spaghetti with the bouillon and tomatoes. You will also need to add an extra ²/₃ cup vegetable bouillon.

This nutritious soup uses split red lentils and carrots as its two main ingredients, and includes a selection of spices to give it an extra kick.

Spicy Dhal *and* Carrot Soup

1 Place the lentils in a large, heavy-bottomed pan with 2½ cups of the vegetable bouillon, the carrots, onions, tomatoes, and garlic. Bring the mixture to a boil over a medium heat, then reduce the heat, cover, and let simmer for 30 minutes, or until the vegetables and lentils are tender.

2 Meanwhile, heat the ghee or vegetable oil in a small pan. over a low heat Add the ground cumin, ground coriander, chili, and turmeric and cook for 1 minute. Remove from the heat and stir in the lemon juice. Season with salt to taste.

3 Working in batches, transfer the soup to a blender or food processor and process until smooth. Return the soup to the pan, add the spice mixture and the remaining 2½ cups of the vegetable bouillon, and let simmer over a low heat for 10 minutes.

4 Add the milk, taste and adjust the seasoning, if necessary. Stir in the chopped cilantro and reheat gently. Ladle the soup into 4 warmed serving bowls with a swirl of yogurt and serve hot.

SERVES 4

¾ cup split red lentils, rinsed and drained
5 cups vegetable bouillon
3 cups carrots, sliced
2 onions, chopped
8 oz/225 g canned chopped tomatoes
2 garlic cloves, chopped
2 tbsp ghee or vegetable oil
1 tsp ground cumin
1 tsp ground coriander
1 fresh green chile, seeded and chopped, or
    1 tsp minced chile
½ tsp ground turmeric
1 tbsp lemon juice
1¼ cups skim milk
2 tbsp chopped fresh cilantro
salt
plain yogurt, to serve

NUTRITION
Calories *173*; Sugars *11 g*; Protein *9 g*;
Carbohydrate *24 g*; Fat *5 g*; Saturates *1 g*

⭐   very easy

🕐   15 mins

🕐   45 mins

For a warming, satisfying meal on a cold day, this lentil dish is packed full of flavor and goodness.

Spicy Lentil Soup

SERVES 4

½ cup split red lentils
2 tsp vegetable oil
1 large onion, chopped finely
2 garlic cloves, minced
1 tsp ground cumin
1 tsp ground coriander
1 tsp garam masala
2 tbsp tomato paste
4 cups vegetable bouillon
12 oz/350 g canned corn, drained
salt and pepper

to serve
lowfat plain yogurt
chopped fresh parsley
warmed pitas

1 Place the split red lentils in a fine strainer and rinse thoroughly under cold running water. Drain well and set side until required.

2 Heat the vegetable oil in a large nonstick skillet over a medium heat. Add the onion and garlic and cook gently until softened, but not browned.

3 Stir in the cumin, coriander, garam masala, tomato paste, and 4 tablespoons of the bouillon. Mix well and let simmer gently for 2 minutes.

4 Add the lentils to the skillet and pour in the remaining vegetable bouillon. Bring to a boil over a medium heat, then reduce the heat, cover, and let simmer for about 1 hour, or until the lentils are tender and the soup thickened. Stir in the corn and heat through for 5 minutes. Season to taste with salt and pepper.

5 Ladle the soup into 4 warmed serving bowls and top each with a spoonful of yogurt and a sprinkling of parsley. Serve immediately with warmed pitas.

NUTRITION
Calories *155*; Sugars *4 g*; Protein *11 g*; Carbohydrate *22 g*; Fat *3 g*; Saturates *0.4 g*

easy
1 hr
1 hr 15 mins

 COOK'S TIP

Many of the ready-prepared ethnic breads available today either contain fat or are brushed with oil before baking. Always check the ingredients list for the fat content before buying.

This is a real winter warmer—pieces of tender beef and chunky mixed vegetables are cooked in a bouillon flavored with dry sherry.

Chunky Potato *and* Beef Soup

1 Heat the vegetable oil in a large pan over a medium heat. Add the strips of steak and cook for 3 minutes, turning constantly.

2 Add the potatoes, carrot, celery, and leeks. Cook, stirring constantly, for an additional 5 minutes.

3 Pour in the beef bouillon and bring to a boil over a medium heat. Reduce the heat until the liquid is simmering gently. Add the sliced baby corn cobs and the bouquet garni envelope.

4 Cook the soup for an additional 20 minutes, or until the meat and the vegetables are tender.

5 Remove the bouquet garni envelope from the pan and discard. Stir the dry sherry into the soup, then season to taste with salt and pepper.

6 Ladle the soup into 4 warmed serving bowls and garnish with chopped parsley. Serve immediately with crusty bread.

SERVES 4

2 tbsp vegetable oil
8 oz/225 g lean braising or frying steak, cut into strips
8 oz/225 g new potatoes, halved
1 carrot, diced
2 celery stalks, sliced
2 leeks, sliced
3¾ cups beef bouillon
8 baby corn cobs, sliced
1 bouquet garni envelope
2 tbsp dry sherry
salt and pepper
chopped fresh parsley, to garnish
crusty bread, to serve

NUTRITION
Calories *187*; Sugars *3 g*; Protein *14 g*; Carbohydrate *12 g*; Fat *9 g*; Saturates *2 g*

⭐⭐   easy

🕐   5 mins

🕐   35 mins

 COOK'S TIP

Make a double quantity of soup and freeze the remainder in a rigid container for later use. When ready to use, place in the refrigerator to thaw thoroughly, then heat until piping hot.

This is a Thai soup, very quickly and easily put together, and cooked so that each ingredient can still be tasted in the finished dish.

Mushroom *and* Ginger Soup

SERVES 4

1 tbsp dried Chinese mushrooms or
    4¹⁄₂ oz/125 g field or crimini mushrooms
4 cups hot vegetable bouillon
¹⁄₄ lb/115 g thread egg noodles
2 tsp corn oil
3 garlic cloves, minced
1-inch/2.5-cm piece fresh gingerroot,
    shredded finely
¹⁄₂ tsp mushroom catsup
1 tsp light soy sauce
1¹⁄₂ cups bean sprouts
fresh cilantro leaves, to garnish

1 Soak the dried Chinese mushrooms (if using) for at least 30 minutes in 1¹⁄₄ cups of the hot vegetable bouillon. Remove and discard the stalks from the fresh mushrooms, then slice. Drain the dried mushrooms and set aside the bouillon.

2 Bring a large pan of water to a boil over a medium heat. Add the noodles and cook for 2–3 minutes. Drain and rinse, then set aside.

3 Heat the corn oil in a large, preheated wok or heavy-bottomed skillet over a high heat. Add the garlic and ginger. Stir and add all the mushrooms and cook for 2 minutes.

4 Add the remaining vegetable bouillon with the reserved bouillon and bring to a boil over a medium heat. Add the mushroom catsup and soy sauce.

5 Stir in the bean sprouts and cook for 1 minute. Place some noodles in 4 serving bowls and ladle the soup on top. Garnish with a few cilantro leaves and serve immediately.

NUTRITION
Calories *74*; Sugars *1 g*; Protein *3 g*;
Carbohydrate *9 g*; Fat *3 g*; Saturates *0.4 g*

easy

1 hr 30 mins

15 mins

 **COOK'S TIP**

Rice noodles contain no fat and are ideal for anyone on a lowfat diet.

Whole young spinach leaves add vibrant color to this unusual soup. Serve with hot, crusty bread for a nutritious light meal.

Yogurt *and* Spinach Soup

1 Pour the chicken bouillon into a large pan. Season to taste with salt and pepper, and bring to a boil over a medium heat. Add the rice and let simmer for 10 minutes until barely cooked. Remove the pan from the heat.

2 Mix the water and cornstarch together to a smooth paste. Pour the yogurt into a second pan and stir in the cornstarch mixture. Set the pan over a low heat and bring the yogurt to a boil, stirring with a wooden spoon in one direction only. This will stabilize the yogurt and prevent it curdling on contact with the hot bouillon. When the yogurt has reached boiling point, stand the pan on a heat diffuser and let simmer for 10 minutes, then remove from the heat and let cool slightly before stirring in the egg yolks.

3 Pour the yogurt mixture into the bouillon, stir in the lemon juice, and stir to blend thoroughly. Keep the soup warm, but do not let it boil.

4 Blanch the washed and drained spinach leaves in a large pan of boiling, salted water for 2–3 minutes, or until they start to soften, but have not wilted. Tip the spinach into a strainer, drain well, and stir into the soup. Warm through. Taste the soup and adjust the seasoning, if necessary. Ladle the soup into 4 wide, shallow soup plates and serve immediately.

SERVES 4

2½ cups chicken bouillon
4 tbsp long-grain rice, rinsed and drained
4 tbsp water
1 tbsp cornstarch
2½ cups lowfat plain yogurt
3 egg yolks, beaten lightly
juice of 1 lemon
12 oz/350 g young spinach leaves, washed and drained
salt and pepper

NUTRITION
Calories 227; Sugars 13 g; Protein 14 g;
Carbohydrate 29 g; Fat 7 g; Saturates 2 g

 moderate

15 mins

 30 mins

This hearty soup uses a variety of green vegetables with a subtle flavoring of ground coriander. A finishing touch of thinly sliced leeks adds texture.

Gardener's Broth

SERVES 4

3 tbsp butter
1 onion, chopped
1–2 garlic cloves, minced
1 large leek
8 oz/225 g Brussels sprouts
¾ cup green beans
5 cups vegetable bouillon
1 cup frozen peas
1 tbsp lemon juice
½ tsp ground coriander
4 tbsp heavy cream
salt and pepper

melba toast
4–6 slices white bread

NUTRITION
Calories *169*; Sugars *5 g*; Protein *4 g*;
Carbohydrate *8 g*; Fat *13 g*; Saturates *5 g*

⭐⭐⭐ moderate

🕐 10 mins

🕐 45 mins

1 Melt the butter in a pan over a low heat. Add the onion and garlic and cook, stirring occasionally, until they start to soften, but not color.

2 Slice the white part of the leek very thinly and set aside. Slice the remaining leek, then slice the Brussels sprouts and thinly slice the beans.

3 Add the green part of the leeks, the Brussels sprouts, and beans to the pan. Add the bouillon and bring to a boil over a medium heat, then reduce the heat and let simmer for 10 minutes. Add the peas, seasoning, lemon juice, and ground coriander. Let simmer for 10–15 minutes, or until the vegetables are tender.

4 Let the soup cool slightly, then transfer to a blender or food processor and process until smooth. Alternatively, rub through a fine strainer with the back of a spoon. Pour into a clean pan.

5 Add the reserved slices of leek to the soup, bring back to a boil, and cook for about 5 minutes, or until the leek is tender. Adjust the seasoning, stir in the cream, and reheat gently.

6 To make the Melba toast, toast the bread on both sides under a preheated hot broiler. Cut horizontally through the slices, then toast the uncooked sides until they curl up. Serve immediately with the soup.

A deep red soup makes a
stunning first course—and
it's easy in the microwave.
A swirl of sour cream gives
a very pretty effect.

Beet *and* Potato Soup

1 Place the onion, potatoes, apple, and water in a large bowl. Cover and cook in the microwave on High power for 10 minutes.

2 Stir in the cumin seeds and cook on High power for 1 minute.

3 Stir in the beet, bay leaf, thyme, lemon juice, and vegetable bouillon. Cover and cook on High power for 12 minutes, stirring halfway through. Set aside, uncovered, for 5 minutes.

4 Remove the bay leaf and discard. Strain the vegetables and set aside the liquid in a pitcher.

5 Place the vegetables with a little of the reserved liquid in a blender or food processor and process until a smooth and creamy purée forms. Alternatively, either mash the vegetable with a potato masher or rub through a strainer.

6 Pour the vegetable purée into a clean bowl with the reserved liquid and mix well. Season to taste with salt and pepper. Cover and cook on High power for 4–5 minutes, or until the soup is piping hot.

7 Ladle the soup into 6 warmed serving bowls. Swirl 1 tablespoon of sour cream into each serving and garnish with a few fresh dill sprigs.

SERVES 4

1 onion, chopped
12 oz/350 g potatoes, diced
1 small cooking apple, peeled, cored, and grated
3 tbsp water
1 tsp cumin seeds
1 lb 2 oz/500 g cooked beet, peeled and diced
1 bay leaf
pinch of dried thyme
1 tsp lemon juice
2½ cups hot vegetable bouillon
4 tbsp sour cream
salt and pepper
fresh dill sprigs, to garnish

NUTRITION
Calories *120*; Sugars *11 g*; Protein *4 g*;
Carbohydrate *22 g*; Fat *2 g*; Saturates *1 g*

 easy

 20 mins

 30 mins

Snacks *and* Appetizers

All too frequently, leaf vegetables are overcooked and limp, with all the goodness and flavor cooked out, while salads are often nothing more than a dismal leaf or two of pale green lettuce with a slice of tomato and a dry ring of onion. Make the most of the wonderful range of fresh produce available in our stores and markets.

Steam broccoli and cabbage so they are colorful and crunchy. Enjoy the wonderfully appetizing shades of orange and yellow bell peppers and the almost unbelievable purple-brown of eggplant. Try grating root vegetables—carrots and daikon—to add flavor and texture to garnishes and casseroles. Look out for red and curly lettuces to bring excitement to an enticing summer salad. Use sweet baby tomatoes in salads and on kabobs, and raid your garden and windowsill for plenty of fresh mint sprigs and basil leaves.

Anyone who loves garlic will adore this dip—it is very potent! Serve it at a barbecue and dip raw vegetables or chunks of French bread into it.

Heavenly Garlic Dip

SERVES 4

2 garlic bulbs
6 tbsp olive oil
1 small onion, chopped finely
2 tbsp lemon juice
3 tbsp sesame seed paste
2 tbsp chopped fresh parsley
salt and pepper
1 fresh Italian parsley sprig, to garnish

to serve
fresh vegetable crudités
French bread or warm pitas

1 Separate the bulbs of garlic into individual cloves. Place them on a cookie sheet and roast in a preheated oven at 400°F/200°C, for 8–10 minutes. Let cool for a few minutes.

2 When they are cool enough to handle, peel the garlic cloves, then chop them finely with a sharp knife.

3 Heat the olive oil in a pan or skillet over a low heat. Add the garlic and onion and sauté, stirring occasionally, for 8–10 minutes, or until softened. Remove the pan or skillet from the heat.

4 Mix in the lemon juice, sesame seed paste, and chopped parsley. Season to taste with salt and pepper. Transfer the dip to a small heatproof bowl and keep warm while you prepare the vegetable crudités.

5 When ready to serve, garnish the dip with a parsley sprig and serve with fresh vegetable crudités, chunks of French bread or warm pitas.

NUTRITION
Calories *344*; Sugars *2 g*; Protein *6 g*;
Carbohydrate *3 g*; Fat *34 g*; Saturates *5 g*

⭐ very easy
🕐 15 mins
🕐 20 mins

👨‍🍳 **COOK'S TIP**

If you come across smoked garlic, use it in this recipe—it tastes wonderful. There is no need to roast the smoked garlic, so omit the first step. This dip can also be used to baste vegetarian burgers.

This wonderful soft cheese pâté is fragrant with the aroma of fresh herbs and garlic. Serve with triangles of Melba toast for a perfect appetizer.

Cheese, Garlic, *and* Herb Pâté

1 Melt the butter in a small skillet over a low heat. Add the garlic and scallions and sauté for 3–4 minutes, or until softened. Let cool.

2 Beat the soft cheese in a large mixing bowl until smooth, then add the garlic and scallions. Stir in the chopped mixed herbs and mix well.

3 Add the cheddar cheese, season to taste with salt and pepper and work the mixture together to form a stiff paste. Cover and chill in the refrigerator until ready to serve.

4 Toast the slices of bread on both sides, then cut off the crusts. Using a sharp bread knife, cut through the slices horizontally to make very thin slices. Cut into triangles, then lightly broil the untoasted sides under a preheated hot broiler until golden.

5 Arrange the mixed salad greens on 4 serving plates with the cherry tomatoes. Pile the cheese pâté on top and sprinkle with a little paprika. Garnish with Italian parsley sprigs and serve with the toast.

SERVES 4

1 tbsp butter
1 garlic clove, minced
3 scallions, chopped finely
1/2 cup full-fat soft cheese
2 tbsp chopped mixed fresh herbs, such as parsley, chives, marjoram, oregano, and basil
1 1/2 cups finely grated sharp cheddar cheese
4–6 slices of white bread from a medium-cut sliced loaf
salt and pepper

to garnish
ground paprika
4 fresh Italian parsley sprigs

to serve
mixed salad greens
cherry tomatoes

NUTRITION
Calories *392*; Sugars *1 g*; Protein *17 g*;
Carbohydrate *18 g*; Fat *28 g*; Saturates *18 g*

easy

20 mins

 10 mins

This delicious smoked fish pâté is given a tart fruity flavor by the gooseberries, which complement the fish perfectly.

Smoked Fish *and* Potato Pâté

SERVES 4

1 lb 7 oz/650 g mealy potatoes, peeled and diced
10½ oz/300 g smoked mackerel, skinned and flaked
3 oz/85 g cooked gooseberries
2 tsp lemon juice
2 tbsp lowfat sour cream
1 tbsp capers, drained
1 gherkin, chopped
1 tbsp chopped dill pickle
1 tbsp chopped fresh dill
salt and pepper
lemon wedges, to garnish
warm crusty bread, to serve

1 Bring a large pan of water to a boil over a medium heat. Add the potatoes and cook for 10 minutes, or until tender, then drain thoroughly.

2 Place the cooked potatoes in a blender or food processor. Add the smoked mackerel and process for 30 seconds, until fairly smooth. Alternatively, place the ingredients in a large bowl and mash with a fork.

3 Add the cooked gooseberries, lemon juice, and sour cream to the fish and potato mixture. Blend for an additional 10 seconds or mash well.

4 Stir in the capers, gherkin, dill pickle, and fresh dill. Season to taste with salt and pepper.

5 Transfer the fish pâté to a serving dish and garnish with lemon wedges. Serve with slices of warm crusty bread.

NUTRITION

Calories *418*; Sugars *4 g*; Protein *18 g*; Carbohydrate *32 g*; Fat *25 g*; Saturates *6 g*

 easy

20 mins

10 mins

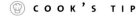 **COOK'S TIP**

Use frozen or canned cooked gooseberries for convenience and to save time, or when fresh gooseberries are out of season.

Red split lentils are used in this spicy recipe for speed as they do not require presoaking. If you use other types of lentil, soak and precook them first according to the package instructions.

Lentil Pâté

1 Heat the vegetable oil in a large pan over a medium heat. Add the onion and garlic and sauté for 2–3 minutes, stirring constantly. Add the spices and cook for an additional 30 seconds. Stir in the vegetable bouillon and lentils and bring the mixture to a boil. Reduce the heat and let simmer for 20 minutes, or until the lentils are cooked. Remove from the heat and drain off any excess moisture.

2 Transfer the mixture to a blender or food processor and add the egg, milk, mango chutney, and parsley. Blend until smooth.

3 Oil and line the bottom of a 1-lb/450-g loaf pan with baking parchment. Spoon the mixture into the pan and level the surface. Cover and cook in a preheated oven at 400°F/200°C, for 40–45 minutes, or until firm.

4 Let the pâté cool in the pan for 20 minutes, then transfer to the refrigerator to cool completely. Turn out onto a serving plate and garnish with parsley sprigs and serve in slices with salad greens and warm toast.

SERVES 4

1 tbsp vegetable oil, plus extra for oiling
1 onion, chopped
2 garlic cloves, minced
1 tsp garam masala
½ tsp ground coriander
3½ cups vegetable bouillon
1 cup red split lentils, washed
1 small egg
2 tbsp milk
2 tbsp mango chutney
2 tbsp chopped fresh parsley
 fresh parsley sprigs, to garnish

to serve
salad greens
warm toast

NUTRITION
Calories *267*; Sugars *12 g*; Protein *14 g*; Carbohydrate *37 g*; Fat *8 g*; Saturates *1 g*

          easy

          25 mins

          1 hr 15 mins

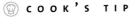 **COOK'S TIP**

Use other spices, such as chili powder or Chinese five-spice powder, to flavor the pâté, and add tomato relish or chili relish instead of the mango chutney, if you prefer.

Tzatziki is a Greek dish,
made with yogurt, mint,
and cucumber. It tastes
superb with warm pitas.

Tzatziki *and* Black Olive Dips

SERVES 4

½ cucumber
1 cup thick unsweetened yogurt
1 tbsp chopped fresh mint
4 pitas
salt and pepper

black olive dip

2 garlic cloves, minced
¾ cup pitted black olives
4 tbsp olive oil
2 tbsp lemon juice
1 tbsp chopped fresh parsley

to garnish

1 fresh mint sprig
1 fresh parsley sprig

1 To make the tzatziki, peel the cucumber and chop coarsely. Sprinkle with salt and let stand for 15–20 minutes. Rinse under cold running water and drain thoroughly.

2 Mix the cucumber, yogurt, and mint together. Season to taste with salt and pepper and transfer to a serving bowl. Cover and chill in the refrigerator for 20–30 minutes.

3 To make the black olive dip, put the minced garlic and olives into a blender or food processor and process for 15–20 seconds. Alternatively, chop them very finely.

4 Add the olive oil, lemon juice, and parsley to the blender or food processor and process for a few more seconds. Alternatively, mix with the chopped garlic and olives and mash together. Season to taste with salt and pepper.

5 Wrap the pitas in aluminum foil and either place over a hot barbecue grill for 2–3 minutes, turning once to warm through, or warm in a preheated oven or under a preheated hot broiler. Cut into pieces and serve with the tzatziki and black olive dips, garnished with mint and parsley sprigs .

NUTRITION
Calories *381*; Sugars *8 g*; Protein *11 g*;
Carbohydrate *52 g*; Fat *15 g*; Saturates *2 g*

very easy

1 hr

3 mins

 **COOK'S TIP**

Sprinkling the cucumber with salt draws out some of its moisture, making it crisper. If you are in a hurry, you can omit this procedure.

Hummus is especially good spread on these garlic toasts for a delicious starter or even as part of a light lunch.

Hummus Toasts *with* Olives

1 To make the hummus, firstly drain the garbanzo beans and set aside 2–3 tablespoons of the liquid. Put the garbanzo beans and half the reserved liquid in a food processor and blend, gradually adding the remaining liquid and lemon juice. Blend well after each addition until smooth.

2 Stir in the sesame seed paste and all but 1 teaspoon of the olive oil. Add the garlic, season to taste with salt and pepper, and blend again until smooth.

3 Spoon the hummus into a serving dish. Drizzle the remaining olive oil over the top and let chill in the refrigerator while preparing the toasts.

4 To make the garlic toasts, lay the ciabatta on a broiler rack in a single layer.

5 Mix the garlic, cilantro, and olive oil together and drizzle over the bread. Cook under a preheated hot broiler for 2–3 minutes, or until golden brown, turning once. To serve, garnish the hummus with chopped cilantro and olives, then serve with the toasts.

SERVES 4

14 oz/400 g canned garbanzo beans
juice of 1 large lemon
6 tbsp sesame seed paste
2 tbsp olive oil
2 garlic cloves, minced
salt and pepper

garlic toasts
1 ciabatta loaf, sliced
2 garlic cloves, minced
1 tbsp chopped fresh cilantro
4 tbsp olive oil

to garnish
1 tbsp chopped fresh cilantro
6 pitted black olives

NUTRITION
Calories *731*; Sugars *2 g*; Protein *22 g*; Carbohydrate *39 g*; Fat *55 g*; Saturates *8 g*

✪✪✪   moderate

🕐   15 mins

🕐   3 mins

Colorful marinated Mediterranean vegetables make a tasty appetizer. Serve with fresh bread or Tomato Toasts (see below).

Bell Pepper Salad

SERVES 4

1 onion
2 red bell peppers
2 yellow bell peppers
3 tbsp olive oil
2 large zucchini, sliced
2 garlic cloves, sliced
1 tbsp balsamic vinegar
1³/₄ oz/50 g canned anchovy fillets, chopped
¹/₄ cup pitted black olives, halved
1 tbsp chopped fresh basil
salt and pepper
4 fresh basil sprigs, to garnish

tomato toasts
1 small stick of French bread
1 garlic clove, minced
1 tomato, peeled and chopped
2 tbsp olive oil

1 Using a sharp knife, cut the onion into wedges. Core and seed the bell peppers, then cut into thick slices.

2 Heat the oil in a large heavy-bottomed skillet over a low heat. Add the onion, bell peppers, zucchini, and garlic and cook gently for about 20 minutes, stirring occasionally.

3 Add the vinegar, anchovies, olives, and chopped basil. Season to taste with salt and pepper. Mix thoroughly and let cool.

4 To make the tomato toasts, cut the French bread diagonally into ¹/₂-inch/1-cm slices.

5 Mix the garlic, tomato, and 1 tablespoon of olive oil together. Season to taste with salt and pepper and spread thinly over each slice of bread.

6 Place the bread on a cookie sheet, drizzle with the remaining olive oil and bake in a preheated oven at 425°F/220°C, for 5–10 minutes, or until crisp. Transfer the salad to 4 serving plates, garnish with basil sprigs and serve with the tomato toasts.

NUTRITION
Calories *234*; Sugars *4 g*; Protein *6 g*;
Carbohydrate *15 g*; Fat *17 g*; Saturates *2 g*

moderate

5–10 mins

35 mins

Using ripe tomatoes and the best extra virgin olive oil will make this Tuscan dish absolutely delicious.

Tuscan Ciabatta

1 Using a sharp knife, cut the cherry tomatoes in half.

2 Using a sharp knife, slice the sun-dried tomatoes into strips.

3 Place the cherry tomatoes and sun-dried tomatoes in a bowl. Add the olive oil and the basil leaves and, using a spoon, toss to mix. Season to taste with a little salt and pepper.

4 Lightly toast the ciabatta slices under a preheated hot broiler.

5 Using a sharp knife, cut the garlic cloves in half, then rub the garlic, cut-side down, over both sides of the toasted ciabatta bread.

6 Transfer the ciabatta bread onto a large serving plate or 4 warmed plates and top with the tomato mixture. Serve immediately.

SERVES 4

10¹/₂ oz/300 g cherry tomatoes
4 sun-dried tomatoes
4 tbsp extra virgin olive oil
16 fresh basil leaves, shredded
8 slices ciabatta
2 garlic cloves
salt and pepper

NUTRITION
Calories *308*; Sugars *3 g*; Protein *7 g*;
Carbohydrate *37 g*; Fat *15 g*; Saturates *2 g*

 ★★★   moderate

🕐 10 mins

🕐 5 mins

 COOK'S TIP

Ciabatta is an Italian rustic bread, which is slightly holey and quite chewy. It is excellent in this recipe, as it absorbs the full flavor of the garlic and extra virgin olive oil.

This colorful fresh salad is delicious at any time of the year. Prosciutto di Parma is thought to be the best ham in the world.

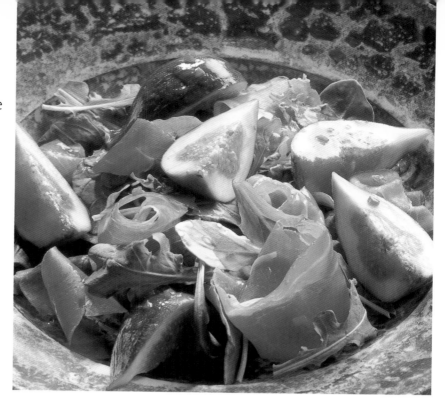

Figs *and* Prosciutto

SERVES 4

1 cup arugula
4 fresh figs
4 slices prosciutto
4 tbsp olive oil
1 tbsp fresh orange juice
1 tbsp honey
1 small fresh red chile

1 Tear the arugula into bite-size pieces, if large, and arrange on 4 large serving plates.

2 Using a sharp knife, cut each of the figs into fourths and place them on top of the arugula.

3 Using a sharp knife, cut the prosciutto into strips and sprinkle over the arugula and figs.

4 Place the oil, orange juice, and honey in a screw-top jar and shake until the mixture emulsifies and forms a thick dressing. Transfer to a small bowl.

5 Using a sharp knife, dice the chile, remembering not to touch your face before you have washed your hands (see Cook's Tip). Add the chopped chili to the dressing and mix well.

6 Drizzle the dressing over the prosciutto, arugula, and figs, tossing to mix well. Serve immediately.

NUTRITION
Calories *121*; Sugars *6 g*; Protein *1 g*;
Carbohydrate *6 g*; Fat *11 g*; Saturates *2 g*

very easy
15 mins
5 mins

🍽 **COOK'S TIP**

Chiles can burn the skin for several hours after chopping, so it is advisable to wear gloves when you are handling the very hot varieties.

Deep-fried seafood is popular all around the Mediterranean, where fish of all kinds is fresh and abundant. Serve with Garlic Mayonnaise and lemon wedges, if you wish.

Crispy Golden Seafood

1 Carefully rinse the squid, shrimp, and whitebait under cold running water, completely removing any accumulated dirt or grit.

2 Using a sharp knife, slice the squid into thick rings but leave the tentacles whole and set aside until required.

3 Heat the oil in a large pan to 350°–375°F/180–190°C, or until a cube of bread browns in 30 seconds.

4 Place the flour in a large bowl and season to taste with the salt, pepper, and the dried basil.

5 Roll the squid, shrimp, and whitebait in the seasoned flour until coated thoroughly all over. Carefully shake off any excess flour.

6 Cook the seafood, in batches, in the hot oil for 2–3 minutes, or until crispy and golden all over. Remove the seafood with a slotted spoon and let drain thoroughly on paper towels.

7 Transfer the deep-fried seafood to 4 large serving plates and serve with the Garlic Mayonnaise (see Cook's Tip).

SERVES 4

7 oz/200 g prepared squid
7 oz/200 g raw jumbo shrimp, shelled
6 oz/150 g oz whitebait
1 cup oil for deep-frying
⅓ cup all-purpose flour
1 tsp dried basil
salt and pepper
Garlic Mayonnaise, to serve (see Cook's Tip)

NUTRITION
Calories *393*; Sugars *0.2 g*; Protein *27 g*;
Carbohydrate *12 g*; Fat *26 g*; Saturates *3 g*

easy

5 mins

15 mins

🍳 COOK'S TIP

To make the Garlic Mayonnaise, mince 2 garlic cloves, stir into 8 tablespoons of mayonnaise, and season to taste with salt and pepper and some chopped fresh parsley. Cover and chill in the refrigerator until ready to serve.

This soup of mussels, cooked in white wine with onions and cream, can be served as an appetizer or a main dish with plenty of crusty bread.

Mussels *in* White Wine

SERVES 4

about 12 cups fresh mussels
¼ cup butter
1 large onion, chopped very finely
2–3 garlic cloves, minced
1½ cups dry white wine
⅔ cup water
2 tbsp lemon juice
good pinch of finely grated lemon peel
1 bouquet garni envelope
1 tbsp all-purpose flour
4 tbsp light or thick cream
2–3 tbsp chopped fresh parsley
salt and pepper
crusty bread, to serve

NUTRITION
Calories *396*; Sugars *2 g*; Protein *23 g*;
Carbohydrate *8 g*; Fat *24 g*; Saturates *15 g*

moderate

5–10 mins

25 mins

1 Pull off all the "beards" from the mussels and scrub them thoroughly under cold running water for about 5 minutes to remove all mud, sand, and barnacles etc. Discard any mussels that refuse to close when sharply tapped with a knife.

2 Melt half the butter in a large pan over a low heat. Add the onion and garlic and cook gently until softened, but not colored.

3 Add the wine, water, lemon juice and peel, and bouquet garni envelope. Season to taste with salt and pepper. Bring to a boil over a low heat, then cover and let simmer for 4–5 minutes.

4 Add the mussels to the pan, cover tightly and let simmer for about 5 minutes, shaking the pan frequently, until all the mussels have opened. Discard any mussels that have not opened. Remove the bouquet garni and discard.

5 Remove the empty half shell from each mussel. Blend the remaining butter with the flour and whisk into the liquid, a little at a time. Let simmer gently for 2–3 minutes, or until slightly thickened.

6 Add the cream and half the parsley to the soup and reheat gently. Adjust the seasoning, if necessary. Ladle the mussels and liquid into 4 large, warmed serving bowls, sprinkle with the remaining parsley, and serve with plenty of warm crusty bread.

Sandwiches are always a welcome snack, but can be mundane. These crisp rolls filled with roasted bell peppers and cheese are absolutely irresistible.

Ciabatta Rolls

1 Slice the ciabatta rolls in half. Heat the olive oil and garlic in a pan over a low heat, then pour the garlic and oil mixture over the cut surfaces of the rolls. Set aside.

2 Halve and seed all the bell peppers, then place, skin-side up, on a broiler rack. Cook under a preheated hot broiler for 8–10 minutes, or until just starting to char. Remove the bell peppers from the broiler and place in a plastic bag, then let cool. When cool enough to handle, peel and slice thinly.

3 Arrange the radish slices on 1 half of each roll with a few arugula leaves. Spoon the cream cheese on top. Pile the roasted bell peppers on top of the cream cheese and top with the other half of the roll. Serve immediately.

SERVES 4

4 ciabatta rolls
2 tbsp olive oil
1 garlic clove, minced

filling

1 red bell pepper
1 green bell pepper
1 yellow bell pepper
4 radishes, sliced
1½ cups arugula
½ cup cream cheese

NUTRITION

Calories *328*; Sugars *6 g*; Protein *8 g*;
Carbohydrate *34 g*; Fat *19 g*; Saturates *9 g*

⭐⭐   easy

🕐   15 mins

🕐   10 mins

 COOK'S TIP

If you do not like the taste of green bell peppers, substitute an orange one instead.

This tasty Chinese appetizer is not all that it seems—the "seaweed" is in fact bok choy, which is deep-fried, salted, and tossed with pine nuts.

Crispy Seaweed

SERVES 4

2 lb 4 oz/1 kg bok choy
3½ cups peanut oil, for deep-frying
1 tsp salt
1 tbsp superfine sugar
2½ tbsp toasted pine nuts

1 Place the bok choy leaves in a strainer and rinse under cold running water. Pat dry thoroughly on paper towels.

2 Discard any tough outer leaves, then roll each bok choy leaf up and, using a sharp knife, slice through very thinly so the leaves are finely shredded. Alternatively, use a food processor to shred the bok choy.

3 Heat the peanut oil in a large preheated wok or heavy-bottomed pan over a medium heat.

4 Carefully add the shredded bok choy leaves to the wok or pan and cook for about 30 seconds, or until they shrivel up and become crispy, resembling seaweed (you will probably need to do this in several batches, depending on the size of your wok or pan).

5 Remove the crispy seaweed from the wok or pan with a slotted spoon and drain on paper towels.

6 Transfer the crispy seaweed to a large bowl and toss with the salt, sugar, and pine nuts. Transfer to 4 warmed serving plates and serve immediately.

NUTRITION
Calories 214; Sugars 14 g; Protein 6 g; Carbohydrate 15 g; Fat 15 g; Saturates 2 g

⭐ very easy

🕐 10 mins

🕐 5 mins

🍳 **COOK'S TIP**

The tough outer leaves of bok choy are discarded as these will spoil the overall taste and texture of the dish. Use savoy cabbage instead of the bok choy if it is unavailable, drying the leaves thoroughly before cooking.

Polenta can be found in most food stores or health food stores. Yellow in color, it acts as a binding agent in this recipe.

Spicy Corn Fritters

1 Place the corn kernels, chiles, garlic, lime leaves, cilantro, egg, and polenta in a large mixing bowl, and stir thoroughly.

2 Add the green beans to the bowl and, using a wooden spoon, mix well.

3 Divide the mixture into small, evenly sized balls, then flatten the balls of mixture gently between the palms of your hands to form rounds.

4 Heat the peanut oil in a large preheated wok or large skillet until really hot. Cook the fritters in batches, turning occasionally, until brown and crispy on the outside.

5 Remove the fritters from the wok or skillet with a slotted spoon and let drain on paper towels while cooking the remaining fritters.

6 Transfer the fritters to 4 warmed serving plates and serve immediately.

SERVES 4

1 cup canned or frozen corn kernels
2 fresh red chiles, seeded and finely chopped
2 garlic cloves, minced
10 kaffir lime leaves, chopped finely
2 tbsp chopped fresh cilantro
1 large egg
½ cup polenta
¾ cup fine green beans, sliced finely
½ cup peanut oil for deep-frying

NUTRITION
Calories *213*; Sugars *6 g*; Protein *5 g*; Carbohydrate *30 g*; Fat *8 g*; Saturates *1 g*

easy

5 mins

15 mins

This classic Chinese appetizer is also great for serving at parties—but be sure to make plenty!

Pork Sesame Toasts

SERVES 4

9 oz/250 g lean pork
²⁄₃ cup raw shrimp, shelled and deveined
4 scallions, trimmed
1 garlic clove, minced
1 tbsp chopped fresh cilantro leaves
    and stems
1 tbsp Thai fish sauce
1 egg
8–10 slices of thick-cut white bread
3 tbsp sesame seeds
²⁄₃ cup vegetable oil
salt and pepper

to garnish
fresh cilantro sprigs
red bell pepper, sliced finely

1 Place the pork, shrimp, scallions, garlic, cilantro, Thai fish sauce, and egg into a blender or food processor. Season to taste with salt and pepper, then process for a few seconds until the ingredients are finely chopped. Transfer the mixture to a bowl. Alternatively, chop the pork, shrimp, and scallions very finely, and mix with the garlic, cilantro, Thai fish sauce, and egg. Season to taste with salt and pepper and mix until blended.

2 Spread the pork and shrimp mixture thickly over the slices of bread so it reaches up to the edges. Cut off the crusts and slice each piece of bread into 4 squares or triangles.

3 Sprinkle the topping liberally with sesame seeds.

4 Heat the vegetable oil in a preheated wok or skillet over a medium heat. Add a few pieces of the bread and cook, topping side down first so the egg sets, for about 2 minutes, or until golden brown. Turn the pieces over to cook on the other side, about 1 minute.

5 Remove the toasts from the wok or skillet and let drain on paper towels. Cook the remaining pieces. Arrange the toasts on a serving plate, garnish with cilantro sprigs and strips of red bell pepper, then serve.

NUTRITION
Calories *674*; Sugars *2 g*; Protein *33 g*;
Carbohydrate *33 g*; Fat *46 g*; Saturates *7 g*

easy

5 mins

35 mins

Chunks of chicken breast are marinated in a mixture of lime juice, garlic, sesame oil, and fresh gingerroot to give them a great flavor.

Sesame Ginger Chicken

1 To make the marinade, place the garlic, shallot, sesame oil, Thai fish sauce or soy sauce, lime or lemon peel and juice, sesame seeds, grated gingerroot and mint in a large non-metallic bowl. Season with a little salt and pepper and stir well until all the ingredients are thoroughly mixed.

2 Remove the skin from the chicken breasts and discard. Using a sharp knife, cut the flesh into chunks.

3 Add the chicken to the marinade, stirring to coat the chicken completely in the mixture. Cover with plastic wrap and chill in the refrigerator for at least 2 hours, so all the flavors are absorbed.

4 Thread the chicken onto 4 presoaked wooden satay sticks. Place them on the rack of a broiler pan and baste with the marinade.

5 Cook the kabobs under a preheated hot broiler for about 8–10 minutes. Turn them frequently, basting them with the remaining marinade.

6 Put the chicken kabobs onto a large serving plate, garnish with a mint sprig and serve immediately with a dipping sauce.

SERVES 4

1 lb 2 oz/500 g boneless chicken breasts
1 fresh mint sprig, to garnish
dipping sauce, to serve

marinade
1 garlic clove, minced
1 shallot, chopped very finely
2 tbsp sesame oil
1 tbsp Thai fish sauce or light soy sauce
finely grated peel of 1 lime or ½ lemon
2 tbsp lime juice or lemon juice
1 tsp sesame seeds
2 tsp finely grated fresh gingerroot
2 tsp chopped fresh mint
salt and pepper

NUTRITION
Calories *204*; Sugars *0 g*; Protein *28 g*;
Carbohydrate *1 g*; Fat *10 g*; Saturates *2 g*

easy

2 hrs 15 mins

10 mins

👑 **COOK'S TIP**

These chicken kabobs taste delicious if they are dipped into an accompanying bowl of hot chili sauce.

For best results, use raw jumbo shrimp in their shells. They are about 3–4 inches/7–10 cm long, and you should get 18–20 per 1 lb 2 oz/500 g.

Spicy Salt *and* Pepper Shrimp

SERVES 4

9-10½ oz/250-300 g raw shrimp in their
    shells, thawed if frozen
1 tbsp light soy sauce
1 tsp Chinese rice wine or dry sherry
2 tsp cornstarch
1 cup vegetable oil, for deep-frying
2–3 scallions, to garnish

spicy salt and pepper
1 tbsp salt
1 tsp ground Szechuan peppercorns
1 tsp Chinese five-spice powder

1 Pull the soft legs off the shrimp, but keep the body shell on. Dry well on paper towels.

2 Place the shrimp in a bowl with the soy sauce, Chinese rice wine or sherry, and cornstarch. Coat the shrimp in the mixture, cover and let marinate in the refrigerator for about 25–30 minutes.

3 To make the spicy salt and pepper, mix the salt, ground Szechuan peppercorns and Chinese five-spice powder together in a small bowl. Place in a dry skillet and cook for 3–4 minutes over a low heat, stirring constantly, to prevent the spices burning on the bottom of the skillet. Remove from the heat and let cool.

4 Heat the vegetable oil in a preheated wok or large skillet until smoking. Add the shrimp, in batches, and deep-fry until golden brown. Remove the shrimp from the wok or skillet with a slotted spoon and let drain on paper towels.

5 Place the scallions in a bowl, pour on 1 tablespoon of the hot oil and let stand for 30 seconds. Transfer the shrimp to a large serving plate and garnish with the scallions. Serve with the spicy salt and pepper as a dip.

NUTRITION
Calories *160*; Sugars *0.2 g*; Protein *17 g*;
Carbohydrate *0.5 g*; Fat *10 g*; Saturates *1 g*

⭐⭐⭐   moderate

🕐   35 mins

🕐   20 mins

👨‍🍳 **COOK'S TIP**

The roasted spice mixture made with Szechuan peppercorns is used throughout China as a dip for deep-fried food. The peppercorns are sometimes roasted first, then ground. Dry-frying releases the flavors of the spices.

Serve as a snack, or simply spread on small pieces of toasted crusty bread (crostini) as an appetizer with drinks.

Crostini *alla* Fiorentina

1 Heat the olive oil in a skillet over a low heat. Add the onion, celery, carrot, and garlic and cook gently for 4–5 minutes.

2 Meanwhile, rinse the chicken livers and pat dry on paper towels. Rinse the calf's or other liver and pat dry. Slice into strips. Add the liver to the skillet and cook gently for a few minutes until the strips are well sealed on all sides.

3 Add half the wine and cook until it has mostly evaporated. Add the rest of the wine, tomato paste, half the parsley, anchovy fillets, bouillon or water, a little salt, and plenty of pepper.

4 Cover the skillet and let simmer, stirring occasionally, for 15–20 minutes, or until tender and most of the liquid has been absorbed.

5 Let the mixture cool slightly, then either coarsely mince or put into a food processor and process to a chunky purée.

6 Return to the skillet and add the butter, capers, and remaining parsley. Heat through gently until the butter melts. Adjust the seasoning, if necessary and spoon into a bowl. Garnish with chopped parsley and serve warm or cold on slices of toasted crusty bread.

SERVES 4

3 tbsp olive oil
1 onion, chopped
1 celery stalk, chopped
1 carrot, chopped
1–2 garlic cloves, minced
4¹⁄₂ oz/125 g chicken livers
4¹⁄₂ oz/125 g calf's, lamb's, or pig's liver
²⁄₃ cup red wine
1 tbsp tomato paste
2 tbsp chopped fresh parsley
3–4 canned anchovy fillets, chopped finely
2 tbsp bouillon or water
2–3 tbsp butter
1 tbsp capers, drained
salt and pepper
chopped fresh parsley, to garnish
small pieces of toasted crusty bread, to serve

NUTRITION
Calories 393; Sugars 2 g; Protein 17 g; Carbohydrate 19 g; Fat 25 g; Saturates 9 g

 moderate

🕐 10 mins

🕐 40–45 mins

In this dish, strips of chicken or beef are threaded onto skewers, broiled and served with a spicy peanut sauce.

Chicken *or* Beef Satay

SERVES 6

4 boneless, skinless chicken breasts or
   1 lb 10 oz/750 g rump steak, trimmed

marinade
1 small onion, chopped finely
1 garlic clove, minced
1-inch/2.5-cm piece fresh gingerroot, grated
2 tbsp dark soy sauce
2 tsp chili powder
1 tsp ground coriander
2 tsp dark brown sugar
1 tbsp lemon or lime juice
1 tbsp vegetable oil

peanut sauce
1¼ cups coconut milk
⅓ cup crunchy peanut butter
1 tbsp Thai fish sauce
1 tsp lemon or lime juice
salt and pepper

NUTRITION
Calories *314*; Sugars *8 g*; Protein *32 g*;
Carbohydrate *10 g*; Fat *16 g*; Saturates *4 g*

---

     moderate
     2 hrs 15 mins
     15 mins

1 Using a sharp knife, trim any fat from the chicken or beef and discard. Cut the meat into thin strips, about 3-inches/7.5-cm long.

2 To make the marinade, place all the ingredients in a large, shallow dish and mix well. Add the meat strips and coat well in the marinade. Cover with plastic wrap and let marinate in the refrigerator for 2 hours, or preferably overnight.

3 Remove the meat from the marinade and thread the pieces, concertina style, onto presoaked bamboo or thin wooden skewers.

4 Place the satays under a preheated medium-hot broiler and cook for 8–10 minutes, turning and brushing occasionally with the marinade, until cooked through.

5 Meanwhile, to make the sauce, mix the coconut milk with the peanut butter, Thai fish sauce, and lemon or lime juice in a pan. Bring to a boil over a low heat and cook for 3 minutes. Season to taste with salt and pepper.

6 Pour the sauce into a serving bowl and serve with the cooked satays and lime wedges.

This is an ideal dish for cooks in a hurry, as it is prepared in minutes from pantry ingredients.

Pasta *and* Anchovy Sauce

1 Set aside 1 teaspoon of the olive oil and heat the remainder in a small pan over a medium heat. Add the garlic and cook for 3 minutes.

2 Reduce the heat, stir in the anchovies and cook, stirring occasionally, until the anchovies have disintegrated.

3 Bring a large pan of lightly salted water to a boil over a medium heat. Add the pasta and the remaining olive oil and cook for 8–10 minutes, or until just done.

4 Add the pesto and chopped oregano to the anchovy mixture, then season with pepper to taste.

5 Drain the pasta thoroughly with a slotted spoon and transfer to a warmed serving dish. Pour the pesto mixture over the pasta and sprinkle over the grated Parmesan cheese.

6 Garnish with fresh oregano sprigs and serve immediately with extra cheese, if you wish.

SERVES 4

6 tbsp olive oil
2 garlic cloves, minced
2 oz/55 g canned anchovy fillets, drained
1 lb/450 g dried spaghetti
2 oz/55 g pesto
2 tbsp finely chopped fresh oregano
1 cup freshly grated Parmesan cheese, plus extra for serving (optional)
salt and pepper
2 fresh oregano sprigs, to garnish

NUTRITION
Calories 712; Sugars 4 g; Protein 25 g; Carbohydrate 81 g; Fat 34 g; Saturates 8 g

 moderate

 10 mins

10 mins

25 mins

COOK'S TIP

If you find canned anchovy fillets rather too salty, soak them in a saucer of cold milk for 5 minutes, drain, and pat dry with paper towels before using. The milk absorbs the salt.

Fish *and* Seafood

The wealth of species and flavors of fish that the world's oceans and rivers provide is immense. Each country combines its local catch with the region's favorite herbs and spices to create a variety of dishes. All of the recipes featured here are easy to prepare and delicious to eat. Moreover, not only are fish and seafood quick to cook, but they are also packed full with nutritional goodness. Naturally low in fat, yet rich in minerals and proteins, fish and seafood are important to help balance any diet.

The superb recipes in this chapter demonstrate the richness of cooking with fish and seafood. Dishes include modern variations of traditional recipes, such as Shrimp Pasta Bake and Trout with Smoked Bacon, and exotic flavors, such as Seafood Chow Mein and Indian Cod with Tomatoes.

Seafood is plentiful in Italy and each region has its own seafood salad. The dressing needs to be chilled for several hours, so prepare well in advance.

Seafood Salad

SERVES 4

2½ cups water
⅔ cup dry white wine
6 oz/175 g squid rings, thawed if frozen
8 oz/225 g hake or angler fish, cut into cubes
16–20 mussels, scrubbed and debearded
20 clams in shells, scrubbed
4½–6 oz/125–175 g raw shrimp, shelled
3–4 scallions sliced (optional)
radicchio and frisée leaves, to serve
lemon wedges, to garnish

dressing
6 tbsp olive oil
1 tbsp wine vinegar
2 tbsp chopped fresh parsley
1–2 garlic cloves, minced
salt and pepper

garlic mayonnaise
5 tbsp thick mayonnaise
2–3 tbsp plain yogurt
2 garlic cloves, minced
1 tbsp capers, drained
2 tbsp chopped fresh parsley or mixed herbs

NUTRITION
Calories *471*; Sugars *2 g*; Protein *34 g*;
Carbohydrate *4 g*; Fat *33 g*; Saturates *5 g*

⭐⭐⭐ moderate
🕐 45–55 mins
🕐 20–22 mins

1 Place the water and wine in a large pan and bring to a boil over a low heat. Add the squid and cook for 5 minutes, or until nearly tender. Add the fish and continue to cook gently for 7–8 minutes, or until tender. Strain and set aside the fish. Pour the bouillon into a clean pan.

2 Bring the fish bouillon to a boil over a medium heat. Add the mussels and clams, cover, and let simmer gently for about 5 minutes, or until the shells open. Discard any mussels that remain closed. Drain the shellfish and remove from their shells, then place in a bowl with the cooked fish. Add the shrimp and scallions (if using).

3 To make the dressing, whisk the olive oil, vinegar, parsley, and garlic together. Season to taste with salt and pepper and pour over the fish, mixing well. Cover and chill in the refrigerator for several hours.

4 To make the mayonnaise, place all the ingredients in a bowl and mix until blended. Cover and chill in the refrigerator until ready to serve.

5 Arrange the radicchio and frisée on 4 large serving plates and spoon the fish salad into the center. Garnish with lemon wedges and serve with the garlic mayonnaise.

🍳 **COOK'S TIP**

You could substitute cooked scallops for the mussels and cockles for the clams, if you prefer.

The colorful combination of chargrilled red bell peppers and mussels makes this an ideal light lunch on a hot summer's day. Serve with plenty of crusty bread.

Mussel Salad

1 Place the bell peppers, skin-side up, on a broiler rack and cook under a preheated hot broiler for 8–10 minutes, or until the skin is charred and blistered and the flesh is soft. Remove from the broiler with tongs, place in a bowl, and cover with plastic wrap. Let cool for about 10 minutes, then peel off the skins.

2 Slice the bell pepper flesh into thin strips and place in a bowl. Gently stir in the shelled mussels.

3 To make the dressing, whisk the olive oil, lemon juice and peel, honey, mustard, and chives together in a bowl until well blended. Season to taste with salt and pepper, then add the bell pepper and mussel mixture and toss gently until coated.

4 Remove the central core of the radicchio and shred the leaves. Place in a serving bowl with the arugula and toss together.

5 Pile the mussel mixture into the center of the leaves and arrange the green-lipped mussels in their shells around the edge of the bowl. Garnish with lemon peel and serve with crusty bread.

SERVES 4

2 large red bell peppers, halved and seeded
12 oz/350 g cooked shelled mussels, thawed if frozen
1 head of radicchio
⅓ cup arugula
8 cooked green-lipped mussels in their shells
strips of lemon peel, to garnish
crusty bread, to serve

dressing

1 tbsp olive oil
1 tbsp lemon juice
1 tsp finely grated lemon peel
2 tsp honey
1 tsp French mustard
1 tbsp snipped fresh chives
salt and pepper

NUTRITION
Calories *181*; Sugars *3.5 g*; Protein *18 g*;
Carbohydrate *11.3 g*; Fat *10.4 g*; Saturates *3 g*

easy

15 mins

10 mins

Small cannellini beans, zucchini, and tomatoes are briefly cooked in a sweet and sour sauce, before being mixed with tuna.

Sweet *and* Sour Tuna Salad

SERVES 4

2 tbsp olive oil

1 onion, chopped

2 garlic cloves, chopped

2 zucchini, sliced

4 tomatoes, peeled

14 oz/400 g canned small cannellini beans, drained and rinsed

10 pitted black olives, halved

1 tbsp capers, drained

1 tsp superfine sugar

1 tbsp whole-grain mustard

1 tbsp white wine vinegar

7 oz/200 g canned tuna, drained

2 tbsp chopped fresh parsley, plus extra to garnish

crusty bread, to serve

1 Heat the olive oil in a large, heavy-bottomed skillet over a low heat. Add the onion and garlic and cook, stirring occasionally, for 5 minutes, or until softened, but not browned.

2 Add the zucchini and cook, stirring occasionally, for an additional 3 minutes.

3 Cut the tomatoes in half, then into thin wedges.

4 Add the tomatoes to the skillet with the small cannellini beans, olives, capers, sugar, mustard, and vinegar.

5 Let simmer for 2 minutes, stirring gently, then let cool slightly.

6 Flake the tuna and stir it into the bean mixture with the chopped parsley. Transfer to 4 serving plates garnish with extra chopped parsley and serve warm with crusty bread.

NUTRITION

Calories *245*; Sugars *5 g*; Protein *22 g*; Carbohydrate *24 g*; Fat *8 g*; Saturates *1 g*

⭐⭐   easy

🕐   15 mins

🕐   10 mins

 COOK'S TIP

Capers are the flower buds of the caper bush, which is native to the Mediterranean region. Capers are preserved in vinegar and salt and give a distinctive flavor to this salad. They are used in Italian and Provençal cooking.

Smoked trout and horseradish are natural partners, but with apple and arugula this makes a wonderful first course.

Smoked Trout *and* Apple Salad

1 Leaving the skin on, cut the apples into fourths and remove the cores. Slice the apples into a bowl and toss in the French dressing to prevent them turning brown.

2 Arrange the arugula on 4 large serving plates.

3 Skin the trout and take out the bone. Carefully remove any fine bones that remain, using your fingers or tweezers. Flake the trout into fairly large pieces and arrange with the apple between the arugula.

4 To make the horseradish dressing, whisk all the ingredients together, adding a little milk if too thick, then drizzle over the trout. Sprinkle the snipped chives and flowers (if using) over the trout and serve with the Melba toast (see Cook's Tip).

SERVES 4

2 orange-red eating apples
2 tbsp French dressing
½ cup arugula
1 smoked trout, about 6 oz/175 g
Melba toast, to serve (see Cook's Tip)

horseradish dressing
½ cup lowfat plain yogurt
½–1 tsp lemon juice
1 tbsp horseradish sauce
milk, optional
salt and pepper

to garnish
1 tbsp snipped fresh chives
fresh chive flowers, optional

NUTRITION
Calories *133*; Sugars *11 g*; Protein *12 g*;
Carbohydrate *11 g*; Fat *5 g*; Saturates *1 g*

⭐ very easy
🕐 10 mins
🕐 20 mins

 COOK'S TIP

To make the Melba toast, toast medium-sliced bread, then cut off the crusts, and slice in half horizontally. Cut in half diagonally and place toasted side down in a warmed oven for 15–20 minutes until the edges start to curl.

Serve as part of a selection of antipasti, or for a summer lunch with hot garlic bread. Tuna and beans make a classic combination.

Tuna, Bean, *and* Anchovy Salad

SERVES 4

1 lb 2 oz/500 g tomatoes
7 oz/200 g canned tuna, drained
2 tbsp chopped fresh parsley
½ cucumber
1 small red onion
8 oz/225 g cooked green beans
1 small red bell pepper, seeded
1 small crisp lettuce
6 tbsp Italian-style dressing
3 hard-cooked eggs
2 oz/55 g canned anchovy fillets, drained
12 pitted black olives

1 Cut the tomatoes into wedges, flake the tuna, and put both into a small bowl with the chopped parsley.

2 Cut the cucumber into slices. Thinly slice the onion, then add the cucumber and onion to the bowl.

3 Cut the green beans in half, chop the bell pepper, and add both to the bowl with the lettuce leaves. Pour over the dressing and toss to mix well, then spoon into a salad bowl. Shell the eggs and cut into fourths. Add to the salad with the anchovies, then sprinkle over the olives and serve.

NUTRITION
Calories *397*; Sugars *8 g*; Protein *23 g*;
Carbohydrate *10 g*; Fat *30 g*; Saturates *4 g*

very easy

20 mins

0 mins

A lemon and herb sauce perfectly complements the sweet flavor and delicate texture of the fish.

Fillets *of* Red Snapper *and* Pasta

1 Place the red snapper fillets in a large casserole. Pour over the wine and add shallots, garlic, herbs, lemon peel and juice, nutmeg, and anchovies. Season to taste with salt and pepper. Cover the casserole and bake in a preheated oven at 350°F/180°C, for 35 minutes.

2 Transfer the baked red snapper fillets carefully to a warmed dish and set aside. Keep warm.

3 Pour the cooking liquid into a pan and bring to a boil over a low heat. Mix the cream and cornstarch together in a small bowl and stir into the sauce to thicken.

4 Meanwhile, bring a large pan of lightly salted water to a boil over a medium heat. Add the pasta and olive oil and cook for 8–10 minutes, or until done. Drain the pasta thoroughly and transfer to a warmed serving dish.

5 Arrange the red snapper fillets on top of the pasta and pour over the sauce. Garnish with a mint sprig, a few slices of lemon, and some strips of lemon peel. Serve immediately.

SERVES 4

2 lb 4 oz/1 kg red snapper fillets
1¼ cups dry white wine
4 shallots, chopped finely
1 garlic clove, minced
3 tbsp finely chopped mixed fresh herbs
finely grated peel and juice of 1 lemon
pinch of freshly grated nutmeg
3 canned anchovy fillets, chopped coarsely
2 tbsp heavy cream
1 tsp cornstarch
1 lb/450 g dried vermicelli
1 tsp olive oil
salt and pepper

to garnish
1 fresh mint sprig
lemon slices
lemon peel

NUTRITION
Calories *457*; Sugars *3 g*; Protein *39 g*; Carbohydrate *44 g*; Fat *12 g*; Saturates *5 g*

★★★ moderate
15 mins
1 hr

🍴 **COOK'S TIP**

If you cannot find red snapper fillets, use whatever fish is available, such as trout.

Most trout available nowadays is farmed rainbow trout. However, if you can, buy wild brown trout for this recipe.

Trout *with* Smoked Bacon

SERVES 4

1 tbsp butter for greasing
4 trout, about 9½ oz/275 g each, gutted and cleaned
12 canned anchovy fillets in oil, drained and chopped
2 apples, peeled, cored and sliced
4 fresh mint sprigs
juice of 1 lemon
12 slices rindless smoked fatty bacon
1 lb/450 g dried tagliatelle
1 tsp olive oil
salt and pepper

to garnish
2 apples, cored and sliced
4 fresh mint sprigs

1 Grease a large cookie sheet with the butter.

2 Open up the cavities of each trout and rinse with warm salt water. Season each cavity with salt and pepper. Divide the anchovies, apples, and mint between each of the cavities, then sprinkle the lemon juice into each cavity.

3 Carefully cover the whole of each trout, except the head and tail, with 3 slices of smoked bacon in a spiral shape.

4 Arrange the trout on the prepared cookie sheet with the loose ends of bacon tucked underneath. Season with pepper to taste and bake in a preheated oven at 400°F/200°C, for about 20 minutes, turning the trout over after 10 minutes.

5 Meanwhile, bring a large pan of lightly salted water to a boil over a medium heat. Add the pasta and olive oil and cook for about 10–12 minutes, or until just done. Drain thoroughly and transfer to a warmed serving dish.

6 Remove the trout from the oven and arrange on top of the pasta. Garnish with sliced apples and mint sprigs, and serve immediately.

NUTRITION
Calories *802*; Sugars *8 g*; Protein *68 g*;
Carbohydrate *54 g*; Fat *36 g*; Saturates *10 g*

 challenging

35 mins

25 mins

Fresh salmon and pasta in a mouthwatering lemon and arugula sauce—a wonderful summer evening treat.

Salmon Steaks *with* Penne

1 Place the salmon in a large skillet and add the butter, wine, sea salt, the peppercorns, dill, tarragon, and lemon. Cover and bring to a boil over a low heat and let simmer for 10 minutes.

2 Using a spatula, carefully remove the salmon. Strain and set aside the cooking liquid. Remove the salmon skin and center bones and discard. Place in a warmed dish, cover and keep warm.

3 Meanwhile, bring a large pan of lightly salted water to a boil over a medium heat. Add the pasta and 1 teaspoon of the olive oil and cook for 12 minutes, or until just done. Drain and sprinkle over the remaining olive oil. Place in a warmed serving dish and top with the salmon steaks. Keep warm.

4 To make the sauce, melt the butter in a small pan over a low heat, then stir in the flour for 2 minutes. Stir in the milk and 7 tablespoons of the reserved cooking liquid. Add the lemon juice and peel and cook, stirring, for an additional 10 minutes.

5 Add the arugula to the sauce and stir gently. Season to taste with salt and pepper.

6 Pour the sauce over the salmon and pasta, then garnish with lemon slices and arugula leaves. Serve immediately.

SERVES 4

4 fresh salmon steaks, about
  10 oz/280 g each
4 tbsp butter
¾ cup dry white wine
pinch of sea salt
8 peppercorns
1 fresh dill sprig
1 fresh tarragon sprig
1 lemon, sliced
4 cups dried penne
1 tbsp olive oil

lemon & arugula sauce
2 tbsp butter
¼ cup all-purpose flour
⅝ cup warm milk
juice and finely grated peel of 2 lemons
1¼ cups arugula, chopped
salt and pepper

to garnish
lemon slices
arugula leaves

NUTRITION
Calories *968*; Sugars *3 g*; Protein *59 g*;
Carbohydrate *49 g*; Fat *58 g*; Saturates *19 g*

⭐⭐   easy
     10 mins
🕐   30 mins

This dish is ideal for an easy family supper. You can use whatever pasta you like, but the tricolor varieties will give the most colorful results.

Shrimp Pasta Bake

SERVES 4

2 cups dried tricolor pasta shapes
1 tbsp vegetable oil
2⅓ cups sliced white mushrooms
1 bunch of scallions, chopped
14 oz/400 g canned tuna in brine, drained and flaked
6 oz/175 g shelled shrimp, thawed if frozen
2 tbsp cornstarch
scant 2 cups skim milk
4 medium tomatoes, sliced thinly
½ cup fresh bread crumbs
¼ cup reduced-fat grated cheddar cheese
salt and pepper

NUTRITION
Calories 723; Sugars 9 g; Protein 56 g;
Carbohydrate 114 g; Fat 8 g; Saturates 2 g

  easy

10 mins

50 mins

1 Bring a large pan of lightly salted water to a boil over a medium heat. Add the pasta and cook for about 8–10 minutes, or until just done. Drain the pasta thoroughly.

2 Meanwhile, heat the vegetable oil in a large skillet over a low heat. Add the mushrooms and all but a handful of the scallions and cook, stirring occasionally, for 4–5 minutes, or until softened.

3 Place the cooked pasta in a small bowl and stir in the mushroom mixture, tuna, and shrimp.

4 Blend the cornstarch with a little milk to make a paste. Pour the remaining milk into a pan and stir in the paste. Heat, stirring, until the sauce starts to thicken. Season to taste with salt and pepper. Stir the sauce into the pasta mixture, then transfer to a casserole and place on a cookie sheet.

5 Arrange the tomato slices over the pasta and sprinkle with the bread crumbs and grated cheese. Bake in a preheated oven at 375°F/190°C, for 25–30 minutes, or until golden. Sprinkle with the reserved scallions and serve immediately.

Use whatever seafood is available for this delicious noodle dish—mussels or crab would be suitable.

Seafood Chow Mein

1 Open up the squid body and score the inside in a criss-cross pattern, then cut into pieces about the size of a postage stamp. Soak the squid in a bowl of boiling water until all the pieces curl up. Rinse in cold water and drain.

2 Cut each scallop into 3–4 slices. Cut the shrimp in half lengthwise, if large. Blend the cornstarch with a little water to make a paste. Mix the scallops and shrimp together with the egg white and cornstarch paste.

3 Bring a large pan of water to a boil over a medium heat. Add the noodles and cook for 5–6 minutes. Drain and rinse under cold running water. Drain again, then toss with about 1 tablespoon of vegetable oil.

4 Heat 3 tablespoons of vegetable oil in a preheated wok over a medium heat. Add the noodles and 1 tablespoon of the soy sauce and cook, stirring, for about 2–3 minutes. Transfer to a large serving dish.

5 Heat the remaining oil in the wok and add the snow peas and seafood. Stir-fry for about 2 minutes, then add the salt, sugar, wine, remaining soy sauce, and about half the scallions. Blend well and add a little bouillon or water if necessary. Pour the mixture on top of the noodles and sprinkle with sesame oil. Garnish with the remaining scallions and serve.

SERVES 4

3 oz/85 g squid body, cleaned
3–4 fresh scallops
3 oz/85 g raw shrimp, shelled
1 tbsp cornstarch
½ egg white, beaten lightly
9½ oz/275 g egg noodles
5–6 tbsp vegetable oil
2 tbsp light soy sauce
½ cup snow peas
½ tsp salt
½ tsp sugar
1 tsp Chinese rice wine
2 scallions, shredded finely
few drops of sesame oil

NUTRITION
Calories *281*; Sugars *1 g*; Protein *15 g*; Carbohydrate *16 g*; Fat *18 g*; Saturates *2 g*

 ⭐⭐⭐ moderate

 🕐 15 mins

🕐 15 mins

👨‍🍳 COOK'S TIP

Chinese rice wine, made from glutinous rice, is also known as "yellow wine" because of its golden amber color. If it is unavailable, a good dry or medium sherry is an acceptable substitute.

This delicious dish combines sweet and sour flavors with the addition of egg, rice noodles, jumbo shrimp, and vegetables for a real treat.

Sweet *and* Sour Noodles

SERVES 4

3 tbsp Thai fish sauce
2 tbsp distilled white vinegar
2 tbsp palm or superfine sugar
2 tbsp tomato paste
2 tbsp corn oil
3 garlic cloves, minced
12 oz/350 g rice noodles, soaked in boiling
  water for 5 minutes
8 scallions, sliced
2 carrots, grated
1½ cups bean sprouts
2 eggs, beaten
8 oz/225 g shelled jumbo shrimp
½ cup chopped peanuts
1 tsp chili flakes, to garnish

1 Mix the Thai fish sauce, vinegar, sugar, and tomato paste together in a small bowl.

2 Heat the corn oil in a large preheated wok over a low heat. Add the garlic and cook for 30 seconds.

3 Drain the noodles thoroughly and add them to the wok together with the fish sauce and tomato paste mixture. Mix well.

4 Add the scallions, carrots, and bean sprouts to the wok and cook for an additional 2–3 minutes.

5 Move the stir-fry mixture to one side of the wok, add the beaten eggs to the empty part of the wok, and cook until the egg sets. Add the shrimp and peanuts to the wok and mix well. Transfer to 4 warmed serving dishes and garnish with chili flakes. Serve immediately.

NUTRITION

Calories *352*; Sugars *14 g*; Protein *23 g*;
Carbohydrate *29 g*; Fat *17 g*; Saturates *3 g*

moderate

10 mins

10 mins

🍳 **COOK'S TIP**

Chili flakes may be found in the spice section of large food stores.

Cellophane or "glass" noodles are made from mung beans. They are sold dried, so they need soaking before use.

Chili Shrimp Noodles

1 Mix the light soy sauce, lime or lemon juice, and Thai fish sauce together in a small bowl. Add the bean curd chunks and toss them until well coated in the mixture. Cover with plastic wrap and set aside for 15 minutes.

2 Place the noodles in a large bowl and pour over enough warm water to cover. Let soak for about 5 minutes, then drain thoroughly.

3 Heat the sesame oil in a preheated wok or large skillet over a low heat. Add the shallots, garlic, and chile, then stir-fry for 1 minute.

4 Add the sliced celery and carrots and stir-fry for an additional 2–3 minutes.

5 Tip the drained noodles into the wok or skillet and cook, stirring constantly, for 2 minutes, then add the small shrimp, bean sprouts, and the bean curd with soy sauce mixture. Cook over a medium-high heat for 2–3 minutes, or until heated through.

6 Transfer the mixture to 4 warmed serving dishes, garnish with celery leaves and chiles, and serve.

SERVES 4

2 tbsp light soy sauce
1 tbsp lime or lemon juice
1 tbsp Thai fish sauce
125 g/4½ oz firm bean curd, cut into chunks (drained weight)
125 g/4½ oz cellophane noodles
2 tbsp sesame oil
4 shallots, sliced finely
2 garlic cloves, minced
1 small fresh red chile, seeded and finely chopped
2 celery stalks, sliced finely
2 carrots, sliced finely
⅔ cup cooked, shelled small shrimp
1 cup bean sprouts

to garnish
celery leaves
fresh chiles

NUTRITION
Calories 152; Sugars 2 g; Protein 11 g; Carbohydrate 10 g; Fat 8 g; Saturates 1 g

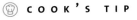 moderate

  25 mins

  10 mins

🍳 **COOK'S TIP**

Try using raw jumbo shrimp instead of the cooked shrimp and add them to the wok with the celery in step 4.

Fish and fruit are tossed with a trio of bell peppers in this spicy dish served with noodles for a quick, healthy meal.

Noodles *with* Cod *and* Mango

SERVES 4

9 oz/250 g egg noodles
1 lb/450 g skinless cod fillet
1 tbsp paprika
2 tbsp corn oil
1 red onion, sliced
1 orange bell pepper, seeded and sliced
1 green bell pepper, seeded and sliced
3½ oz/100 g baby corn cobs, halved
1 mango, peeled, pitted, and sliced
1 cup bean sprouts
2 tbsp tomato catsup
2 tbsp soy sauce
2 tbsp medium sherry
1 tsp cornstarch

1 Place the egg noodles in a large bowl and pour over enough boiling water to cover. Let stand for about 10 minutes.

2 Rinse the cod fillet under cold running water and pat dry with paper towels. Cut the cod flesh into thin strips, then place in a large bowl. Add the paprika and toss well to coat the fish.

3 Heat the corn oil in a large preheated wok over a medium heat. Add the onion, bell peppers, and baby corn cobs and cook for about 5 minutes.

4 Add the cod to the wok together with the sliced mango and cook for an additional 2–3 minutes, or until the fish is tender. Add the bean sprouts and toss well.

5 Mix the tomato catsup, soy sauce, sherry, and cornstarch together in a small bowl. Add the mixture to the wok and cook, stirring occasionally, until the juices thicken.

6 Drain the noodles thoroughly and transfer to 4 warmed serving bowls. Transfer the cod and mango stir-fry to separate warmed serving bowls and serve immediately.

NUTRITION
Calories *274*; Sugars *11 g*; Protein *25 g*;
Carbohydrate *26 g*; Fat *8 g*; Saturates *1 g*

easy

10 mins

25 mins

Chicken and noodles are cooked, then tossed in an oyster sauce and egg mixture in this recipe.

Oyster Sauce Noodles

1 Place the egg noodles in a large bowl or dish and pour over enough boiling water to cover. Let stand for 10 minutes.

2 Meanwhile, remove the skin from the chicken thighs and discard. Cut the chicken flesh into small pieces with a sharp knife.

3 Heat the peanut oil in a large preheated wok or skillet, swirling the oil around the bottom of the wok until it is really hot.

4 Add the chicken pieces and the carrot to the wok or skillet and cook for about 5 minutes.

5 Drain the noodles thoroughly, then add to the wok or skillet and cook for an additional 2–3 minutes, or until the noodles are heated through.

6 Beat the oyster sauce, eggs, and cold water together in a small bowl. Drizzle the mixture over the noodles and cook for an additional 2–3 minutes, or until the eggs set.

7 Transfer the mixture to 4 warmed serving bowls and serve immediately.

SERVES 4

9 oz/250 g egg noodles
1 lb/450 g chicken thighs
2 tbsp peanut oil
1 large carrot, sliced
3 tbsp oyster sauce
2 eggs
3 tbsp cold water

NUTRITION
Calories *278*; Sugars *2 g*; Protein *30 g*;
Carbohydrate *13 g*; Fat *12 g*; Saturates *3 g*

⭐⭐ easy

🕐 5 mins

🕐 25 mins

 COOK'S TIP

Flavor the eggs with soy sauce or hoisin sauce as an alternative to the oyster sauce, if you prefer.

One of those easy, delicious meals where the rice and fish are cooked together in one pan. Make sure the whole spices are removed before serving.

Aromatic Seafood Rice

SERVES 4

1¼ cups basmati rice
2 tbsp ghee or vegetable oil
1 onion, chopped
1 garlic clove, minced
1 tsp cumin seeds
½–1 tsp chili powder
4 cloves
1 cinnamon stick or a piece of cassia bark
2 tsp curry paste
8 oz/225 g shelled shrimp
1 lb 2 oz/500 g white fish fillets (such as angler fish, cod or haddock), skinned and boned, and cut into bite-size pieces
2½ cups boiling water
⅓ cup frozen peas
⅓ cup frozen corn kernels
1–2 tbsp lime juice
2 tbsp toasted shredded coconut
salt and pepper

to garnish
1 fresh cilantro sprig
2 lime slices

NUTRITION

Calories *380*; Sugars *2 g*; Protein *40 g*;
Carbohydrate *26 g*; Fat *13 g*; Saturates *5 g*

moderate

20 mins

25 mins

1 Place the rice in a fine strainer and wash well under cold running water until the water runs clear. Drain thoroughly.

2 Heat the ghee or vegetable oil in a pan over a low heat. Add the onion, garlic, spices, and curry paste and cook very gently for 1 minute.

3 Stir in the rice and mix well until coated in the spiced oil. Add the shrimp and white fish, then season well with salt and pepper. Stir lightly, then pour in the boiling water.

4 Cover and cook for 10 minutes. Add the peas and corn, cover and cook for an additional 8 minutes. Remove from the heat and let stand for 10 minutes.

5 Uncover the pan, fluff up the rice with a fork, and transfer to a large, warmed serving platter.

6 Sprinkle the dish with the lime juice and toasted coconut, and garnish with a cilantro sprig and 2 lime slices. Serve immediately.

Quick and easy—cod steaks are cooked in a rich tomato and coconut sauce to produce tender, succulent results.

Indian Cod *with* Tomatoes

1 Heat the vegetable oil in a skillet over a medium heat. Add the fish steaks and season to taste with salt and pepper. Cook until browned on both sides, but not cooked through. Remove from the skillet and set aside.

2 Add the onion, garlic, red bell pepper, and spices and cook very gently for about 2 minutes, stirring frequently. Add the tomatoes, bring to a boil and let simmer for 5 minutes.

3 Add the fish steaks to the skillet and let simmer gently for 8 minutes, or until the fish is cooked through.

4 Remove the fish from the skillet and keep warm in a serving dish. Add the coconut milk and cilantro or parsley to the skillet and reheat gently.

5 Spoon the sauce over the fish and serve immediately.

SERVES 4

3 tbsp vegetable oil
4 cod steaks, about 1-inch/2.5-cm thick
1 onion, chopped finely
2 garlic cloves, minced
1 red bell pepper, seeded and chopped
1 tsp ground coriander
1 tsp ground cumin
1 tsp ground turmeric
½ tsp garam masala
14 oz/400 g canned chopped tomatoes
⅔ cup coconut milk
1–2 tbsp chopped fresh cilantro or parsley
salt and pepper

NUTRITION
Calories *194*; Sugars *6 g*; Protein *21 g*;
Carbohydrate *7 g*; Fat *9 g*; Saturates *1 g*

 easy

 5 mins

⏱ 25 mins

🍴 **COOK'S TIP**

The mixture may be flavored with 1 tablespoon of curry powder or curry paste (mild, medium, or hot, according to personal preference) instead of the mixture of spices in step 2, if you wish.

The moist texture of the broiled flounder is complemented by the texture of the mushrooms.

Flounder *with* Mushrooms

SERVES 4

4 flounder fillets, about 150 g/5½ oz each
2 tbsp lime juice
⅓ cup lowfat spread
2½ cups mixed small mushrooms such as white, oyster, shiitake, chanterelle, or morel, sliced or cut into fourths
4 tomatoes, peeled, seeded, and chopped
celery salt and pepper
fresh basil leaves, to garnish
mixed salad greens, to serve

1 Line a broiler rack with baking parchment and place the fish on top.

2 Sprinkle over the lime juice and season to taste with celery salt and pepper.

3 Place under a preheated medium-hot broiler and cook for 7–8 minutes without turning, until just cooked. Keep warm.

4 Meanwhile, gently melt the lowfat spread in a skillet over a low heat. Add the mushrooms and cook for 4–5 minutes, or until cooked through.

5 Gently heat the tomatoes in a small pan over a low heat.

6 Transfer the fish to 4 large, warmed serving plates and spoon over the mushrooms, with any pan juices, and the tomatoes. Garnish with a few basil leaves and serve with mixed salad greens.

NUTRITION
Calories *243*; Sugars *2 g*; Protein *30 g*;
Carbohydrate *2 g*; Fat *13 g*; Saturates *3 g*

easy

10 mins

20 mins

COOK'S TIP

Mushrooms are ideal in a lowfat diet, as they are packed full of flavor and contain no fat. "Meatier" types of mushroom, such as crimini, will take slightly longer to cook.

The firm, sweet flesh of the fresh trout is enhanced by the spicy flavor of the marinade.

Delicately Spiced Trout

1 Using a sharp knife, slash the trout skin in several places on both sides.

2 To make the marinade, mix all the ingredients together in a bowl.

3 Place the trout in a large, shallow dish and pour the marinade over. Cover and let marinate in the refrigerator for about 30–40 minutes, turning the fish occasionally.

4 Heat the corn oil in a preheated wok or Balti pan over a medium heat. Add the fennel seeds and onion seeds and cook until they start popping.

5 Add the garlic, coconut milk, and tomato paste, then bring the mixture to a boil over a medium heat.

6 Add the golden raisins, garam masala, and trout with the juices from the marinade. Cover and let simmer for 5 minutes. Turn the trout over carefully and let simmer for an additional 10 minutes.

7 Transfer the trout to 4 warmed serving plates and garnish with cashews, lemon wedges and cilantro sprigs. Serve immediately.

SERVES 4

4 trout, about 6–9 oz/175–250 g
   each, cleaned
3 tbsp corn oil
1 tsp fennel seeds
1 tsp onion seeds
1 garlic clove, minced
2/3 cup coconut milk or fish bouillon
3 tbsp tomato paste
1/3 cup golden raisins
1/2 tsp garam masala

marinade
4 tbsp lemon juice
2 tbsp chopped fresh cilantro
1 tsp ground cumin
1/2 tsp salt
1/2 tsp ground black pepper

to garnish
1/4 cup chopped cashews
lemon wedges
4 fresh cilantro sprigs

NUTRITION
Calories 374; Sugars 13 g; Protein 38 g;
Carbohydrate 14 g; Fat 19 g; Saturates 3 g

 easy

50 mins

 20 mins

The combination of fresh and smoked fish gives these kabobs a very special flavor. Try to choose thick fish fillets for good, bite-size chunks.

Smoky Fish Kabobs

SERVES 4

12 oz/350 g smoked cod fillet
12 oz/350 g cod fillet
8 large raw shrimp
8 bay leaves
fresh dill sprigs, to garnish (optional)

marinade
4 tbsp corn oil, plus a little for brushing
2 tbsp lemon or lime juice
grated peel of ½ lemon or lime
¼ tsp dried dill
salt and pepper

1 Skin both types of cod and cut the flesh into bite-size pieces. Shell the shrimp, leaving the tails intact.

2 To make the marinade, mix the corn oil, lemon or lime juice and peel, dried dill, and seasoning together in a shallow, non-metallic dish.

3 Place the prepared fish in the marinade and stir well until the fish is coated on all sides. Cover and let marinate in the refrigerator for 1–4 hours.

4 Thread the fish onto 4 metal skewers, alternating the fish with the shrimp and bay leaves.

5 Cover the barbecue grill rack with lightly oiled aluminum foil. Place the fish kabobs on top and cook over hot coals on a hot barbecue for 5–10 minutes, basting with any remaining marinade. Turn once.

6 Transfer the kabobs to a warmed serving plate, garnish with fresh dill, if you wish, and serve immediately.

NUTRITION
Calories *221*; Sugars *0 g*; Protein *33 g*;
Carbohydrate *0 g*; Fat *10 g*; Saturates *1 g*

easy
10 mins, plus 1–4 hrs
5–10 mins

 COOK'S TIP

Cod fillet can be rather flaky, so choose the thicker end, which is easier to cut into chunky pieces. Cook the fish on foil rather than directly on the rack, so that if the fish breaks away from the skewer, it is not wasted.

Since the scallops are marinated, it is not essential that they are live. Thawed frozen shellfish will work well in this recipe.

Scallop Kabobs

1 If using wooden skewers, soak 8 of them in warm water for at least 30 minutes before you use them. This prevents the skewers burning on the barbecue.

2 Mix the lime peel and juice, lemongrass, garlic, and chile together in a mortar with a pestle to make a paste. Alternatively, use a spice grinder.

3 Thread 2 scallops onto each of the presoaked skewers. Cover the ends with a piece of aluminum foil to prevent them burning.

4 Alternate the scallops with the lime segments.

5 To make the dressing, whisk the corn oil and lemon juice together, then season to taste with salt and pepper.

6 Coat the scallops with the prepared spice paste and cook for 10 minutes over a medium-hot barbecue grill, basting occasionally. Turn the skewers once.

7 Toss the arugula, mixed salad greens, and dressing together, then transfer to a large serving bowl and garnish with chives.

8 Serve the scallops piping hot, 2 skewers on each plate, with the salad.

SERVES 4

grated peel and juice of 2 limes
2 tbsp finely chopped lemongrass or
    1 tbsp lemon juice
2 garlic cloves, minced
1 fresh green chile, seeded and chopped
16 scallops, with corals
2 limes, each cut into 8 segments
2 tbsp corn oil
1 tbsp lemon juice
salt and pepper
fresh chives, to garnish

to serve
1 cup arugula salad
3 cups mixed salad greens

NUTRITION
Calories *182*; Sugars *0 g*; Protein *29 g*;
Carbohydrate *0 g*; Fat *7 g*; Saturates *1 g*

easy

30 mins

10 mins

Meat Dishes

Many of the meat dishes on offer may be classic and traditional, but they are all speedy to make, and use ingredients that can be pantry staples. Others have a modern twist, but are equally simple to prepare.

The dishes in this chapter range from easy, economic midweek suppers to quick but sophisticated and elegant main courses for special occasions. All these recipes are extremely wholesome, offering a comprehensive range of flavors. Those on a lowfat diet should use lean cuts and look out for lowfat ground meat to enjoy the dishes featured here.

This quick and easy dish tastes superb and would make a delicious treat for a special occasion.

Creamed Strips *of* Short Loin

SERVES 4

6 tbsp butter
1 lb/450 g short loin steak, trimmed and
    cut into thin strips
1½ cups sliced white mushrooms
1 tsp mustard
pinch of freshly grated gingerroot
2 tbsp dry sherry
⅔ cup heavy cream
salt and pepper
4 slices hot toast, cut into triangles, to serve

pasta

1 lb/450 g dried rigatoni
2 tsp olive oil
2 fresh basil sprigs
½ cup butter

1 Melt the butter in a large skillet over a low heat. Add the steak and cook, stirring frequently, for 6 minutes. Using a slotted spoon, transfer the steak to an ovenproof dish and keep warm.

2 Add the sliced mushrooms to the skillet and cook for 2–3 minutes in the juices remaining in the skillet. Add the mustard and ginger, then season to taste with salt and pepper. Cook for 2 minutes, then add the sherry and cream. Cook for an additional 3 minutes, then pour the sauce over the steak.

3 Bake the steak and sauce in a preheated oven at 375°F/ 190°C, for 10 minutes.

4 Meanwhile, bring a large pan of lightly salted water to a boil over a medium heat. Add the pasta, olive oil, and 1 of the basil sprigs, and cook for 10 minutes, or until just done. Drain the pasta thoroughly and transfer to a warmed serving dish. Toss the pasta with the butter and garnish with the other basil sprig.

5 Serve the steak with the pasta and triangles of hot toast.

NUTRITION
Calories *796*; Sugars *2 g*; Protein *29 g*;
Carbohydrate *26 g*; Fat *63 g*; Saturates *39 g*

easy

15 mins

30 mins

🍲 **COOK'S TIP**

Dried pasta will keep for up to 6 months. Keep it in the package and reseal it once you have opened it, or transfer the pasta to an airtight jar.

Any variety of long pasta, such as fettuccine or tagliatelle, could be used for this very tasty dish from Sicily.

Sicilian Spaghetti Cake

1 Brush an 8-inch/20-cm loose-bottomed circular cake pan with a little olive oil, then place a disc of baking parchment in the bottom, and brush with oil. Trim the eggplant and cut into slanting slices, 1/4-inch/5-mm thick. Heat some of the olive oil in a skillet over a medium heat. Add a few slices of eggplant at a time and cook until lightly browned on both sides. Add more oil, as necessary. Drain on paper towels.

2 Put the ground beef, onion, and garlic into a pan and cook over a low heat, stirring frequently, until browned all over. Add the tomato paste, tomatoes, Worcestershire sauce, and herbs. Season to taste with salt and pepper. Simmer gently for 10 minutes, stirring occasionally, then add the olives and bell pepper and cook for an additional 10 minutes.

3 Bring a large pan of lightly salted water to a boil over a medium heat. Add the pasta and cook for 8–10 minutes, or until just done. Drain it thoroughly and transfer to a bowl. Add the meat mixture and Parmesan cheese and toss together with 2 forks.

4 Arrange the eggplant in overlapping slices over the bottom and up the sides of the cake pan. Add the meat and cover with the remaining eggplant slices.

5 Stand the cake pan in a baking pan and cook in a preheated oven at 400°F/200°C, for 40 minutes. Remove from the oven, let stand for 5 minutes, then loosen around the edges and invert onto a warmed serving dish. Remove the baking parchment and discard, then serve immediately.

SERVES 4

2/3 cup olive oil, plus extra for brushing
2 eggplant
generous 3 cups finely ground lean beef
1 onion, chopped
2 garlic cloves, minced
2 tbsp tomato paste
14 oz/400 g canned chopped tomatoes
1 tsp Worcestershire sauce
1 tsp chopped fresh oregano or marjoram or 1/2 tsp dried oregano or marjoram
1/2 cup pitted black olives, sliced
1 green, red, or yellow bell pepper, seeded and chopped
6 oz/175 g dried spaghetti
generous 1 cup freshly grated Parmesan cheese
salt and pepper

NUTRITION
Calories 876; Sugars 10 g; Protein 37 g; Carbohydrate 39 g; Fat 65 g; Saturates 18 g

⭐⭐ easy

🕐 30 mins

 50 mins

The combination of Italian and Indian ingredients makes a surprisingly delicious recipe. Marinate the steak in advance to save time and garnish with fresh cilantro and slivered almonds, if you wish.

Beef *and* Pasta Bake

S E R V E S   4

2 lb/900 g steak, cut into cubes
²⁄₃ cup beef bouillon
1 lb/450 g dried macaroni
1¼ cups heavy cream
½ tsp garam masala
salt
fresh cilantro , to garnish

korma paste

½ cup blanched almonds
6 garlic cloves
3 tsp coarsely chopped fresh gingerroot
6 tbsp beef bouillon
1 tsp ground cardamom
4 cloves, ground
1 tsp ground cinnamon
2 large onions, chopped
1 tsp coriander seeds
2 tsp ground cumin seeds
pinch of cayenne pepper
6 tbsp corn oil

N U T R I T I O N
Calories *1050*; Sugars *4 g*; Protein *47 g*;
Carbohydrate *37 g*; Fat *81 g*; Saturates *34 g*

easy
6 hrs 15 mins
1 hr 15 mins

1 To make the korma paste, using a mortar and pestle, grind the almonds finely. Put the ground almonds and the remaining korma paste ingredients into a blender or food processor and process to make a very smooth paste.

2 Place the steak in a large, shallow dish and spoon over the korma paste, turning to coat the steak well. Let marinate in the refrigerator for at least 6 hours.

3 Transfer the steak and korma paste to a large pan and let simmer over a low heat, adding a little beef bouillon, if required, for 35 minutes.

4 Meanwhile, bring a large pan of lightly salted water to a boil over a medium heat. Add the macaroni and cook for 10 minutes, or until just done. Drain thoroughly and transfer to a deep casserole. Add the steak, cream, and garam masala.

5 Bake in a preheated oven at 400°F/ 200°C, for 30 minutes, or until the steak is tender. Remove the casserole from the oven and let stand for 10 minutes. Garnish the bake with fresh cilantro leaves and slivered almonds, if you wish and serve immediately.

A different twist is given to this traditional pasta dish with a rich but subtle sauce.

Meatballs *in* Red Wine Sauce

1 Pour the milk into a bowl, add the bread crumbs, and let soak for 30 minutes.

2 Heat half the butter and 4 tablespoons of the olive oil in a skillet over a low heat. Add the mushrooms and cook for 4 minutes, then stir in the flour and cook for 2 minutes. Stir in the beef bouillon and wine, then let simmer for about 15 minutes. Add the tomatoes, tomato paste, sugar, and basil. Season to taste with salt and pepper and let simmer for 30 minutes.

3 Mix the shallots, steak, and paprika with the bread crumbs and season to taste. Shape the mixture into 14 meatballs.

4 Heat 4 tablespoons of the remaining olive oil and the remaining butter in a large skillet over a medium heat. Add the meatballs and cook, turning frequently, until browned all over. Transfer to a deep casserole, pour over the sauce, cover and bake in a preheated oven at 350°F/180°C, for 30 minutes.

5 Bring a large pan of lightly salted water to a boil over a medium heat. Add the pasta and the remaining olive oil and cook for 8–10 minutes, or until done. Drain and transfer to a serving dish. Remove the casserole from the oven and let cool for 3 minutes, then pour the meatballs and sauce onto the pasta. Garnish with a basil sprig and serve.

SERVES 4

⅔ cup milk
2 cups white bread crumbs
2 tbsp butter
9 tbsp olive oil
3 cups sliced oyster mushrooms
¼ cup whole-wheat flour
⅞ cup beef bouillon
⅔ cup red wine
4 tomatoes, peeled and chopped
1 tbsp tomato paste
1 tsp brown sugar
1 tbsp finely chopped fresh basil
12 shallots, chopped
4 cups ground steak
1 tsp paprika
1 lb/450 g dried egg tagliarini
salt and pepper
1 fresh basil sprig, to garnish

NUTRITION
Calories *811*; Sugars *7 g*; Protein *30 g*;
Carbohydrate *76 g*; Fat *43 g*; Saturates *12 g*

    moderate
   45 mins
   1 hr 30 mins

The fresh taste of sage is the perfect ingredient to counteract the richness of pork in this quick and simple dish.

Pork Chops *with* Sage

SERVES 4

2 tbsp flour
1 tbsp chopped fresh sage or 1 tsp dried sage
4 boneless lean pork chops, trimmed
    of excess fat
2 tbsp olive oil
1 tbsp butter
2 red onions, sliced into rings
1 tbsp lemon juice
2 tsp superfine sugar
4 plum tomatoes, cut into fourths
salt and pepper
salad greens, to serve

1 Mix the flour, sage, and salt and pepper to taste on a large plate. Lightly dust the pork chops on both sides with the seasoned flour.

2 Heat the olive oil and butter in a large skillet over a medium heat. Add the pork chops and cook for 6–7 minutes on each side, or until cooked through. Drain the pork chops and set aside the pan juices. Keep warm.

3 Toss the onion in the lemon juice and add to the skillet. Cook with the sugar and tomatoes for 5 minutes until tender.

4 Transfer the pork chops to 4 warmed serving plates and pour over the pan juices. Serve with the tomato and onion mixture and salad greens.

NUTRITION
Calories 364; Sugars 5 g; Protein 34 g;
Carbohydrate 14 g; Fat 19 g; Saturates 7 g

          easy

                10 mins

                15 mins

This unusual and attractive dish is extremely delicious. Make the Italian Red Wine Sauce (see page 15) well in advance to reduce the preparation time.

Pasta *and* Pork in Cream Sauce

1 Using a meat mallet or the end of a rolling pin, pound the slices of pork between 2 sheets of plastic wrap until wafer thin, then cut into strips.

2 Heat the olive oil in a large skillet over a medium heat. Add the pork and stir-fry for 5 minutes. Add the mushrooms and cook for an additional 2 minutes.

3 Pour over the Italian red wine sauce (see page 15), reduce the heat, and let simmer gently for 20 minutes.

4 Meanwhile, bring a large pan of lightly salted water to a boil over a medium heat. Add the lemon juice, saffron, and pasta and cook for about 8–10 minutes, or until just done. Drain thoroughly and keep warm.

5 Stir the cream into the skillet with the pork and heat for a few minutes.

6 Bring a small pan of water to a boil over a medium heat. Add the eggs and boil for 3 minutes, then cool them in cold water and remove the shells.

7 Transfer the pasta to a large, warmed serving plate, top with the pork, the sauce, and garnish with the eggs. Serve immediately.

SERVES 4

1 lb/450 g pork tenderloin, sliced thinly
4 tbsp olive oil
2 cups sliced white mushrooms
7/8 cup Italian Red Wine Sauce (see page 15)
1 tbsp lemon juice
pinch of saffron
3 cups dried orecchioni
4 tbsp heavy cream
12 quail eggs (see Cook's Tip)
salt

COOK'S TIP

In this recipe, the quail eggs are soft-cooked. As they are extremely difficult to shell when warm, it is important that they are thoroughly cooled first. Otherwise, they will break up unattractively.

NUTRITION
Calories 735; Sugars 4 g; Protein 31 g;
Carbohydrate 37 g; Fat 52 g; Saturates 19 g

moderate

8 hrs 45 mins

35 mins

The addition of juniper berries and fennel to the pork chops gives an unusual and delicate flavor to this dish.

Citrus Pork Chops

SERVES 4

½ fennel bulb
1 tbsp juniper berries, crushed lightly
about 2 tbsp olive oil
finely grated peel of 1 orange
4 pork chops, about 150 g/5½ oz each
juice of 1 orange
crisp salad greens, to serve

1 Using a sharp knife, finely chop the fennel bulb. Discard the tough outer leaves and the feathery fronds.

2 Grind the juniper berries in a mortar with a pestle. Mix the crushed juniper berries with the fennel flesh, olive oil, and orange peel.

3 Using a sharp knife, score a few cuts over each pork chop.

4 Place the pork chops in a roasting pan or an ovenproof dish, then spoon the fennel and juniper mixture over the pork chops.

5 Carefully pour the orange juice over the top of each pork chop, cover, and let marinate in the refrigerator for about 2 hours.

6 Cook the pork chops under a preheated hot broiler for 10–15 minutes, depending on the thickness of the meat, turning occasionally, until the meat is tender and cooked through.

7 Transfer the pork chops to 4 large, warmed serving plates and serve immediately with crisp salad greens.

NUTRITION
Calories 274; Sugars 0 g; Protein 38.4 g;
Carbohydrate 0 g; Fat 13.9 g; Saturates 3 g

⭐⭐ easy

2 hrs 15 mins

10–15 mins

 COOK'S TIP

Juniper berries are most commonly associated with gin, but they are often added to meat dishes in Italy for a delicate sharp flavor. They can be bought dried from most health food stores and some larger supermarkets.

This is a simplified version of a traditional dish from the Marche region, on the east coast of Italy. Pork fillet pockets are stuffed with prosciutto and herbs.

Pork *with* Lemon and Garlic

1 Using a sharp knife, cut the pork fillet into 4 equal pieces. Place the pork between 2 sheets of oiled paper and pound each piece with a meat mallet or the end of a rolling pin to flatten it.

2 Cut a horizontal slit in each piece of pork to make a pocket.

3 Place the almonds on a baking sheet and lightly toast under a preheated medium-hot broiler for 2–3 minutes, or until golden.

4 Mix the almonds with 1 tablespoon of the olive oil, prosciutto, garlic, oregano, and the finely grated peel from 1 lemon. Spoon the mixture into the pockets of the pork.

5 Heat the remaining olive oil in a large skillet over a medium heat. Add the shallots and cook for 2 minutes.

6 Add the pork to the skillet and cook for 2 minutes on each side, or until browned all over.

7 Add the bouillon to the skillet and bring to a boil over a medium heat. Cover and let simmer for 45 minutes, or until the pork is tender. Remove the meat from the skillet, then set aside and keep warm.

8 Add the remaining lemon peel and sugar to the skillet, then boil for about 3–4 minutes, or until reduced and syrupy. Transfer the pork to 4 warmed serving plates and pour over the sauce. Serve immediately with snow peas.

SERVES 4

1 lb/450 g pork fillet
²/₃ cup chopped almonds
2 tbsp olive oil
4 oz/115 g prosciutto, chopped finely
2 garlic cloves, chopped
1 tbsp chopped fresh oregano
finely grated peel of 2 lemons
4 shallots, chopped finely
¾ cup ham or chicken bouillon
1 tsp sugar
freshly cooked snow peas, to serve

NUTRITION
Calories *428*; Sugars *2 g*; Protein *31 g*;
Carbohydrate *4 g*; Fat *32 g*; Saturates *4 g*

 easy

25 mins

1 hr

Chunks of tender lamb, pan-fried with garlic and stewed in red wine is a traditional Roman dish.

Lamb *and* Anchovies *with* Thyme

SERVES 4

1 tbsp olive oil

1 tbsp butter

1 ½ lb/700 g lamb (shoulder or leg), cut in 1-inch/2.5-cm chunks

4 garlic cloves

3 fresh thyme sprigs, stalks removed

6 canned anchovy fillets

²⁄₃ cup red wine

²⁄₃ cup lamb or vegetable bouillon

1 tsp sugar

16 pitted black olives, halved

2 tbsp chopped fresh parsley, to garnish

1 Heat the olive oil and butter in a large skillet over a medium heat. Add the lamb and cook for 4–5 minutes, stirring, until the meat is browned all over.

2 Grind the garlic, thyme, and anchovies together in a mortar with a pestle to make a smooth paste.

3 Add the wine and lamb bouillon to the skillet. Stir in the garlic and anchovy paste together with the sugar.

4 Bring the mixture to a boil over a medium heat, then reduce the heat, cover, and let simmer for about 30–40 minutes, or until the lamb is tender. For the last 10 minutes of the cooking time, remove the lid to let the sauce reduce slightly.

5 Stir the olives into the sauce and mix well.

6 Transfer the lamb and the sauce to a large, warmed serving bowl and garnish with chopped parsley. Serve immediately.

NUTRITION

Calories *299*; Sugars *1 g*; Protein *31 g*; Carbohydrate *1 g*; Fat *16 g*; Saturates *7 g*

moderate

15 mins

50 mins

A classic combination of flavors, this dish would make a perfect Sunday lunch. Serve with a tomato and onion salad and baked potatoes.

Lamb Chops *with* Rosemary

1 Trim the lamb chops by cutting away the flesh with a sharp knife to expose the tips of the bones.

2 Place the oil, lemon juice, garlic, lemon pepper, and salt in a large, shallow, non-metallic dish and mix with a fork.

3 Lay the rosemary sprigs in the dish and place the lamb on top. Let marinate in the refrigerator for at least 1 hour, turning the lamb chops once.

4 Remove the lamb chops from the marinade and wrap a piece of aluminum foil around the bones to stop them burning on the barbecue.

5 Place the rosemary sprigs on a grill rack and place the lamb on top. Cook on a hot barbecue over hot coals for 10–15 minutes, turning once.

6 Meanwhile, make the salad and dressing. Arrange the tomatoes on a serving dish and sprinkle the scallions on top. Place all the ingredients for the dressing in a screw-top jar, shake well, and pour over the salad. Serve with the barbecued lamb chops and baked potatoes.

SERVES 4

8 lamb chops
5 tbsp olive oil
2 tbsp lemon juice
1 garlic clove, chopped finely
½ tsp lemon pepper
salt
8 fresh rosemary sprigs
baked potatoes, to serve

salad

4 tomatoes, sliced
4 scallions, sliced diagonally

dressing

2 tbsp olive oil
1 tbsp lemon juice
1 garlic clove, chopped
¼ tsp chopped fresh rosemary

NUTRITION
Calories *560*; Sugars *1 g*; Protein *48 g*;
Carbohydrate *1 g*; Fat *40 g*; Saturates *1 g*

 moderate

 1 hr 15 mins

 15 mins

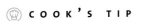 **COOK'S TIP**

Choose medium to small baking potatoes if you want to cook baked potatoes on the grill. Scrub them well, prick with a fork, and wrap in buttered aluminum foil. Bury them in the hot coals and cook for 50–60 minutes.

These lamb chops quickly become more elegant when the bone is removed to make noisettes.

Lamb *with* Bay *and* Lemon

SERVES 4

4 lamb chops
1 tbsp olive oil
1 tbsp butter
²⁄₃ cup white wine
²⁄₃ cup lamb or vegetable bouillon
2 bay leaves
pared peel of 1 lemon
salt and pepper

1 Using a sharp knife, carefully remove the bone from each lamb chop, keeping the meat intact. Alternatively, ask the butcher to prepare the lamb noisettes for you.

2 Shape the meat into rounds and secure with a length of string.

3 Heat the olive oil and butter together in a large skillet over a medium heat until the mixture starts to froth.

4 Add the lamb noisettes to the skillet and cook for 2–3 minutes on each side, or until browned all over.

5 Remove the skillet from the heat, drain off all of the excess fat, and discard.

6 Return the skillet to the heat. Add the wine, bouillon, bay leaves, and lemon peel to the skillet and cook for 20–25 minutes, or until the lamb is tender. Season the lamb noisettes and sauce to taste with a little salt and pepper.

7 Transfer to 4 large, warmed serving plates. Remove the string from each noisette, discard the bay leaves, and serve with the sauce.

NUTRITION
Calories *268*; Sugars *0.2 g*; Protein *24 g*;
Carbohydrate *0.2 g*; Fat *16 g*; Saturates *7 g*

moderate

10 mins

35 mins

The appearance of the leg of lamb as it is opened out to cook on the barbecue grill gives this dish its name.

Butterfly Lamb *with* Mint

1 Open out the boned leg of lamb so its shape resembles a butterfly, then thread 2–3 metal skewers through the meat to make it easier to turn on the barbecue grill.

2 Mix the balsamic vinegar, lemon peel and juice, corn oil, chopped mint, garlic, and sugar together in a non-metallic dish large enough to hold the lamb. Season to taste with salt and pepper.

3 Place the lamb in the dish and turn until it is coated on both sides with the marinade. Let marinate in the refrigerator for at least 6 hours, or preferably overnight, turning occasionally.

4 Remove the lamb from the marinade and set aside the liquid for basting.

5 Place the grill rack about 6 inches/15 cm above the coals on a hot barbecue and grill the lamb for about 30 minutes on each side, turning once and basting frequently with the marinade.

6 Transfer the lamb to a chopping board and remove the skewers. Cut the lamb into slices across the grain and transfer to 4 warmed serving plates. Serve with broiled vegetables with olives and fresh salad greens.

SERVES 4

boned leg of lamb, about 4 lb/1.8 kg
8 tbsp balsamic vinegar
grated peel and juice of 1 lemon
²/₃ cup corn oil
4 tbsp chopped fresh mint
2 garlic cloves, minced
2 tbsp light brown sugar
salt and pepper

to serve
broiled vegetables with olives
salad greens

NUTRITION
Calories *733*; Sugars *6 g*; Protein *69 g*;
Carbohydrate *6 g*; Fat *48 g*; Saturates *13 g*

⭐⭐ easy

🕐 10 mins, plus 6 hrs

 1 hr

This truly spectacular dish is equally delicious whether you use veal or pork fillet. Make sure the roses are free of blemishes and pesticides.

Veal *in a* Rose Petal Sauce

SERVES 4

1 lb/450 g dried fettuccine
6 tbsp olive oil
1 tsp chopped fresh oregano
1 tsp chopped fresh marjoram
3/4 cup butter
1 lb/450 g veal fillet, sliced thinly
2/3 cup rose petal vinegar (see Cook's Tip)
2/3 cup fish bouillon
1/4 cup grapefruit juice
1/4 cup heavy cream
salt

to garnish
12 pink grapefruit segments
12 pink peppercorns
rose petals, washed
fresh herb leaves

1 Bring a large pan of lightly salted water to a boil over a medium heat. Add the pasta and cook for 8–10 minutes, or until just done. Drain the pasta thoroughly and transfer to a warmed serving dish, and sprinkle over 2 tablespoons of the olive oil, the oregano, and marjoram.

2 Heat 4 tablespoons of the butter with the remaining olive oil in a large skillet over a low heat. Add the veal and cook for 6 minutes. Remove the veal from the skillet and place on top of the pasta. Keep warm.

3 Add the vinegar and fish bouillon to the skillet and bring to a boil over a medium heat. Boil vigorously until reduced by two thirds. Add the grapefruit juice and cream, reduce the heat and let simmer for 4 minutes. Dice the remaining butter and add to the skillet, a piece at a time, whisking constantly until it has been incorporated.

4 Pour the sauce around the veal, garnish with grapefruit segments, pink peppercorns, rose petals and your favorite herb leaves, and serve.

NUTRITION
Calories *475*; Sugars *3.6 g*; Protein *39 g*;
Carbohydrate *104 g*; Fat *52 g*; Saturates *16 g*

⭐⭐   easy

🕐   20 mins

🕐   25 mins

 COOK'S TIP

To make the rose petal vinegar, infuse the petals of 8 pesticide-free roses in 2/3 cup white wine vinegar for 48 hours. Prepare well in advance to reduce the preparation time.

The delicious combination of apple, onion, and mushroom perfectly complements the delicate flavor of the veal.

Neapolitan Veal Chops

1 Melt 4 tablespoons of the butter in a skillet over a low heat. Add the veal and cook for 5 minutes on each side. Transfer to a dish and keep warm.

2 Add the onion and apples to the skillet and cook until lightly browned. Transfer to a dish, then place the veal on top and keep warm.

3 Melt the remaining butter in the skillet over a low heat. Add the mushrooms, tarragon, and peppercorns and cook gently for 3 minutes. Sprinkle over the sesame seeds.

4 Bring a large pan of lightly salted water to a boil over a medium heat. Add the pasta and 1 teaspoon of the olive oil and cook until just done. Drain thoroughly and transfer to an ovenproof serving plate.

5 Cook the tomatoes and basil leaves under a preheated hot broiler for about 2–3 minutes. Dot the pasta with the mascarpone and sprinkle with the remaining olive oil. Place the onions, apples, and veal chops on top, then spoon the mushrooms and peppercorns over with the pan juices. Season to taste with salt and pepper. Place the tomatoes and basil leaves around the edge and cook in a preheated oven at 300°F/150°C, for 5 minutes.

6 Transfer to 4 large, warmed serving plates and serve immediately.

SERVES 4

7/8 cup butter
4 veal chops, about 8 oz/225 g each, trimmed
1 large onion, sliced
2 apples, peeled, cored, and sliced
6 oz/175 g white mushrooms
1 tbsp chopped fresh tarragon
8 black peppercorns
1 tbsp sesame seeds
14 oz/400 g dried marille pasta
scant 1/2 cup extra virgin olive oil
3/4 cup mascarpone cheese
2 large beefsteak tomatoes, cut in half
leaves of 1 fresh basil sprig
salt and pepper

NUTRITION
Calories 1071; Sugars 13 g; Protein 74 g;
Carbohydrate 66 g; Fat 59 g; Saturates 16 g

⭐⭐⭐⭐ challenging

🕑 20 mins

🕐 45 mins

This dish is delicious if made with tender veal. However, if veal is unavailable, use pork or turkey escalopes instead.

Veal Italienne

SERVES 4

5 tbsp butter
1 tbsp olive oil
1½ lb/675 g potatoes, peeled and cubed
4 veal escalopes, about 6 oz/175 g each
1 onion, cut into 8 wedges
2 garlic cloves, minced
2 tbsp all-purpose flour
2 tbsp tomato paste
⅔ cup red wine
1¼ cups chicken bouillon
8 ripe tomatoes, peeled, seeded, and diced
8–9 pitted black olives, halved
2 tbsp chopped fresh basil
salt and pepper
fresh basil leaves, to garnish

1 Heat the butter and olive oil in a large skillet over a medium heat. Add the potato cubes and cook for about 5–7 minutes, stirring frequently, until they start to brown.

2 Remove the potatoes from the skillet with a slotted spoon and set aside.

3 Place the veal in the skillet and cook for 2–3 minutes on each side until sealed. Remove from the skillet and set aside.

4 Add the onion and garlic to the skillet and cook for 2–3 minutes.

5 Add the flour and tomato paste and cook for 1 minute, stirring. Gradually blend in the red wine and chicken bouillon, stirring constantly, to make a smooth sauce.

6 Return the potatoes and veal to the skillet. Stir in the tomatoes, olives, and chopped basil, then season to taste with salt and pepper.

7 Transfer to a casserole dish and cook in a preheated oven at 350°F/180°C, for 1 hour, or until the potatoes and veal are cooked through. Transfer to 4 warmed serving plates, garnish with basil leaves, and serve.

NUTRITION

Calories 592; Sugars 5 g; Protein 44 g; Carbohydrate 48 g; Fat 23 g; Saturates 9 g

⭐⭐⭐   moderate

🍳   25 mins

🕐   1 hr 20 mins

🍽 **COOK'S TIP**

For a quicker cooking time and really tender meat, place the meat between 2 sheets of oiled paper and pound with a meat mallet or the end of a rolling pin to flatten it slightly before cooking.

Anchovies are often used to enhance flavor, particularly in meat dishes. Either veal or turkey escalopes can be used for this pan-fried dish.

Escalopes *and* Italian Sausage

1 Heat the olive oil in a large skillet over a medium heat. Add the anchovies, capers, fresh rosemary, grated orange peel and juice, Italian sausage, and tomatoes and cook for 5–6 minutes, stirring occasionally.

2 Meanwhile, place the veal or turkey veal escalopes between 2 sheets of oiled paper and pound with a meat mallet or the end of a rolling pin to flatten.

3 Add the meat to the mixture in the skillet. Season to taste with salt and pepper, cover, and cook for 3–5 minutes on each side, slightly longer if the meat is thicker.

4 Transfer to 4 warmed serving plates and serve with cooked polenta.

SERVES 4

1 tbsp olive oil
6 canned anchovy fillets, drained
1 tbsp capers, drained
1 tbsp fresh rosemary, stalks removed
finely grated peel and juice of 1 orange
3 oz/75 g Italian sausage, diced
3 tomatoes, peeled and chopped
4 veal or turkey escalopes, about 4 oz/ 115 g each
salt and pepper
cooked polenta, to serve

NUTRITION
Calories *233*; Sugars *1 g*; Protein *28 g*; Carbohydrate *1 g*; Fat *13 g*; Saturates *1 g*

 **COOK'S TIP**

Try using 4-minute steaks, slightly flattened, instead of the turkey or veal. Cook them for 4–5 minutes on top of the sauce in the skillet.

 easy

10 mins

20 mins

Poultry

For the poultry-lover there are pasta dishes, broils, and bakes in this chapter, incorporating a variety of healthy and colorful ingredients. For those who enjoy Italian cuisine, there is a number of rich Italian sauces and old favorites including more traditional casseroles, such as Rich Chicken Casserole and Chicken Cacciatora. All of these recipes are mouthwatering and quick and easy to prepare. They are also extremely wholesome, offering a comprehensive range of tastes.

There is a delicious surprise of creamy herb and garlic soft cheese hidden inside these chicken packets!

Garlic *and* Herb Chicken

SERVES 4

4 chicken breasts, skinned
3½ oz/100g full-fat soft cheese, flavored with herbs and garlic
8 slices prosciutto
⅔ cup red wine
⅔ cup chicken bouillon
1 tbsp brown sugar
salad greens, to serve

1 Using a sharp knife, make a horizontal slit along the length of each chicken breast to form a pocket.

2 Place the cheese in a small bowl and beat with a wooden spoon to soften it. Spoon the cheese into the pocket of the chicken breasts.

3 Wrap 2 slices of prosciutto around each chicken breast and secure in place with a length of string.

4 Pour the wine and chicken bouillon into a large skillet and bring to a boil over a medium heat. When the mixture is just starting to boil, add the sugar and stir to dissolve.

5 Add the chicken breasts to the mixture in the skillet. Let simmer for about 12–15 minutes, or until the chicken is tender and the juices run clear when the point of a sharp knife is inserted into the thickest part of the meat.

6 Remove the chicken from the skillet, then set aside and keep warm.

7 Reheat the sauce and boil until reduced and thickened. Remove the string from the chicken and cut into slices. Pour the sauce over the chicken and serve with salad greens.

NUTRITION
Calories 272; Sugars 4 g; Protein 29 g; Carbohydrate 4 g; Fat 13 g; Saturates 6 g

easy

30 mins

25 mins

🍳 COOK'S TIP

Try adding 2 finely chopped sun-dried tomatoes to the soft cheese in step 2, if you prefer.

This casserole is packed with the sunshine flavors of Italy. The sun-dried tomatoes add a wonderful richness to the dish.

Rich Chicken Casserole

1 Place the chicken in a large, heavy-bottomed skillet and cook without fat over a fairly high heat, turning occasionally, until golden brown. Using a slotted spoon, drain off any excess fat from the chicken and transfer to an ovenproof casserole.

2 Heat the olive oil in the skillet over a medium heat. Add the onion, garlic, and bell pepper and cook for 3–4 minutes, then transfer to the casserole.

3 Add the orange peel and juice, chicken bouillon, chopped tomatoes, and sun-dried tomatoes to the casserole and mix well.

4 Bring to a boil, then cover the casserole with a lid and let simmer very gently over a low heat for about 1 hour, stirring occasionally. Add the chopped thyme and olives, then season to taste with salt and pepper.

5 Spoon the chicken casserole onto 4 warmed serving plates, garnish with orange peel and thyme, and serve with crusty bread.

SERVES 4

8 chicken thighs
2 tbsp olive oil
1 medium red onion, sliced
2 garlic cloves, minced
1 large red bell pepper, sliced thickly
thinly pared peel and juice of 1 small orange
½ cup chicken bouillon
14 oz/400 g canned chopped tomatoes
½ cup sun-dried tomatoes, sliced thinly
1 tbsp chopped fresh thyme
16–18 cup pitted black olives
salt and pepper
crusty bread, to serve

to garnish
orange peel
4 fresh thyme sprigs

NUTRITION
Calories *320*; Sugars *8 g*; Protein *34 g*;
Carbohydrate *8 g*; Fat *17 g*; Saturates *4 g*

 moderate

 15 mins

1 hr 15 mins

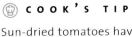 **COOK'S TIP**

Sun-dried tomatoes have a dense texture and concentrated taste, and add intense flavor to slow-cooking casseroles.

Spinach ribbon noodles, topped with a rich tomato sauce and creamy chicken, make an appetizing dish.

Pasta *with* Chicken Sauce

SERVES 4

9 oz/250 g fresh green tagliatelle
1 tsp olive oil
salt and pepper
fresh basil leaves, to garnish

tomato sauce

2 tbsp olive oil
1 small onion, chopped
1 garlic clove, chopped
14 oz/400 g canned chopped tomatoes
2 tbsp chopped fresh parsley
1 tsp dried oregano
2 bay leaves
2 tbsp tomato paste
1 tsp sugar

chicken sauce

4 tbsp sweet butter
14 oz/400 g boned chicken breasts, skinned
   and cut into thin strips
¾ cup blanched almonds
1¼ cups heavy cream

NUTRITION

Calories *995*; Sugars *8 g*; Protein *36 g*;
Carbohydrate *50 g*; Fat *74 g*; Saturates *34 g*

⭐⭐⭐   moderate

🕑   15 mins

🕐   45 mins

1 To make the tomato sauce, heat the olive oil in a pan over a medium heat. Add the onion and cook until translucent. Add the garlic and cook for 1 minute. Stir in the tomatoes, parsley, oregano, bay leaves, tomato paste, and sugar. Season to taste with salt and pepper, bring to a boil, and let simmer, uncovered, for 15–20 minutes, until reduced by half. Remove the pan from the heat and discard the bay leaves.

2 To make the chicken sauce, gently melt the butter in a skillet over a medium heat. Add the chicken and almonds and stir-fry for 5–6 minutes, or until the chicken is cooked through.

3 Meanwhile, bring the cream to a boil in a small pan over a low heat and boil for about 10 minutes, until reduced by almost half. Pour the cream over the chicken and almonds, stir, and season to taste with salt and pepper. Set aside and keep warm.

4 Bring a large pan of lightly salted water to a boil over a medium heat. Add the pasta and olive oil and cook for 8–10 minutes, or until just done. Drain thoroughly and transfer to a warmed serving dish. Spoon over the tomato sauce and arrange the chicken sauce down the center. Garnish with a few basil leaves and serve immediately.

All the sunshine colors and flavors of the Mediterranean are combined in this easy dish.

Chicken Pepperonata

1 Remove the skin from the chicken thighs and toss in the flour.

2 Heat the olive oil in a wide skillet over a high heat. Add the chicken and sauté quickly until sealed and lightly browned, then remove from the skillet. Add the onion to the skillet and gently cook until soft. Add the garlic, bell peppers, tomatoes, and oregano, then bring to a boil, stirring constantly.

3 Arrange the chicken over the vegetables, then season well with salt and pepper. Cover the skillet tightly and let simmer for 20–25 minutes, or until the chicken is tender and the juices run clear when the point of a sharp knife in inserted into the thickest part of the meat.

4 Season to taste, then transfer the chicken to a large serving dish. Garnish with oregano leaves and serve immediately.

SERVES 4

8 skinless chicken thighs
2 tbsp whole-wheat flour
2 tbsp olive oil
1 small onion, sliced thinly
1 garlic clove, minced
1 each large red, yellow, and green bell peppers, sliced thinly
14 oz/400 g canned chopped tomatoes
1 tbsp chopped oregano
salt and pepper
fresh oregano leaves, to garnish

NUTRITION
Calories 328; Sugars 7 g; Protein 35 g; Carbohydrate 13 g; Fat 15 g; Saturates 4 g

	easy
	15 mins
	40 mins

🍳 **COOK'S TIP**

For extra flavor, halve the bell peppers and cook under a preheated hot broiler until the skins are charred. Let cool, then remove the skins and seeds. Slice the bell peppers thinly and use in the recipe.

The refreshing combination of chicken and orange sauce makes this a perfect dish for a warm summer evening.

Chicken *with* Orange Sauce

SERVES 4

2 tbsp canola oil
2 tbsp olive oil
4 skinless, boneless chicken breasts, about
    8 oz/225 g each
⅔ cup brandy
2 tbsp all-purpose flour
⅔ cup freshly squeezed orange juice
¼ cup zucchini, cut into thin batons
¼ red bell pepper, cut into thin batons
6 tbsp leek, shredded finely
14 oz/400 g dried whole-wheat spaghetti
3 large oranges, peeled and cut
    into segments
peel of 1 orange, cut into very fine strips
2 tbsp chopped fresh tarragon
⅔ cup ricotta cheese
salt and pepper
fresh tarragon leaves, to garnish

1 Heat the canola oil and 1 tablespoon of the olive oil in a skillet over a fairly high heat. Add the chicken and cook until golden brown. Add the brandy and cook for 3 minutes. Sprinkle in the flour and cook, stirring constantly, for about 2 minutes.

2 Reduce the heat and add the orange juice, zucchini, red bell pepper, and leek. Season to taste with salt and pepper and let simmer for 5 minutes, or until the sauce has thickened.

3 Meanwhile, bring a large pan of lightly salted water to a boil over a medium heat. Add the pasta and cook for 10 minutes, or until just done. Drain thoroughly, transfer to a warmed serving dish, and drizzle over the remaining olive oil.

4 Add half the orange segments, half the orange peel, the tarragon, and ricotta cheese to the chicken in the skillet and cook, stirring, for 3 minutes.

5 Place the chicken on top of the pasta, pour over a little orange sauce, and garnish with the remaining orange segments and peel. Serve immediately with any extra sauce.

NUTRITION
Calories 797; Sugars 28 g; Protein 59 g;
Carbohydrate 77 g; Fat 25 g; Saturates 6 g

moderate

15 mins

25 mins

These unusual chicken kabobs have a wonderful Italian flavor, and the bacon helps keep them moist during cooking.

Skewered Chicken Spirals

1 Spread out a chicken breast between 2 sheets of plastic wrap and beat firmly with a rolling pin to flatten the chicken to an even thickness. Repeat with the remaining chicken breasts.

2 Mix the garlic and tomato paste together and spread over the chicken. Lay a bacon strip over each, then sprinkle with the basil. Season to taste with salt and pepper.

3 Roll up each piece of chicken firmly, then cut into thick slices.

4 Thread the slices onto 4 metal skewers, making sure the skewer holds the chicken in a spiral shape.

5 Brush lightly with vegetable oil and cook on a hot barbecue grill or under a preheated hot broiler for about 10 minutes, turning once. Serve immediately with salad greens.

SERVES 4

4 skinless, boneless chicken breasts
1 garlic clove, minced
2 tbsp tomato paste
4 strips smoked back bacon
large handful of fresh basil leaves
2 tbsp vegetable oil for brushing
salt and pepper
salad greens, to serve

NUTRITION
Calories *231*; Sugars *1 g*; Protein *29 g*;
Carbohydrate *1 g*; Fat *13 g*; Saturates *5 g*

easy

15 mins

10 mins

A rich caramelized sauce, flavored with balsamic vinegar and wine, gives this chicken dish a piquant flavor.

Chicken *with* Balsamic Vinegar

SERVES 4

4 boned chicken thighs
2 garlic cloves, minced
¾ cup red wine
3 tbsp white wine vinegar
1 tbsp olive oil
1 tbsp butter
4 shallots
3 tbsp balsamic vinegar
2 tbsp fresh thyme
salt and pepper
cooked polenta or rice, to serve

1 Using a sharp knife, make a few slashes in the skin of the chicken. Brush the chicken with the minced garlic and place in a large, shallow dish.

2 Pour the red wine and white wine vinegar over the chicken, then season to taste with salt and pepper. Cover with plastic wrap and let marinate in the refrigerator overnight.

3 Remove the chicken thighs with a slotted spoon, draining well, and set aside the marinade.

4 Heat the olive oil and butter in a skillet over a medium heat. Add the shallots and cook for 2–3 minutes, or until they start to soften.

5 Add the chicken thighs to the skillet and cook for 3–4 minutes, turning, until browned all over. Reduce the heat and add half of the reserved marinade. Cover and cook for 15–20 minutes, adding more marinade when necessary.

6 Once the chicken is tender, add the balsamic vinegar and thyme, then cook for an additional 4 minutes.

7 Transfer the chicken and juices to 4 warmed serving plates and serve immediately with cooked polenta or rice.

NUTRITION
Calories *148*; Sugars *0.2 g*; Protein *11 g*; Carbohydrate *0.2 g*; Fat *8 g*; Saturates *3 g*

 COOK'S TIP

To make the chicken thighs look neater, use wooden skewers to hold them together or secure them with a length of string.

⭐⭐ easy

🍳 2 hrs 10 mins

🕐 35 mins

Olives are a popular flavoring for poultry and game in the Apulia region of Italy, where this recipe originally comes from.

Chicken *with* Green Olives

1 Heat the olive oil and butter in a large skillet over a medium heat. Add the chicken breasts and cook until golden brown all over, then remove the chicken from the skillet with a slotted spoon.

2 Add the onion and garlic to the skillet and cook over a medium heat until starting to soften. Add the bell peppers and mushrooms and cook for about 2–3 minutes. Add the tomatoes and season to taste with salt and pepper. Transfer the vegetables to a casserole and arrange the chicken on top.

3 Add the wine to the skillet and bring to a boil over a medium heat. Pour the wine over the chicken. Cover and cook the casserole in a preheated oven at 350°F/180°C, for 50 minutes.

4 Add the olives to the casserole and mix in. Pour in the cream, cover, and return to the oven for an additional 10–20 minutes.

5 Meanwhile, bring a large pan of lightly salted water to a boil over a medium heat. Add the pasta and cook until just done. Drain the pasta thoroughly and transfer to a warmed serving dish.

6 Serve the chicken straight from the casserole with chopped parsley and the pasta served separately. Alternatively, arrange the chicken on top of the pasta, spoon over the sauce and garnish with parsley, then serve.

SERVES 4

2 tbsp olive oil
2 tbsp butter
4 part boned chicken breasts
1 large onion, chopped finely
2 garlic cloves, minced
2 red, yellow, or green bell peppers, cored, seeded, and cut into large pieces
4 cups sliced white mushrooms
2 tomatoes, peeled and halved
5/8 cup dry white wine
1 1/2 cups pitted green olives
4–6 tbsp heavy cream
14 oz/400 g dried pasta
salt and pepper
chopped fresh Italian parsley, to garnish

NUTRITION

Calories *614*; Sugars *6 g*; Protein *34 g*;
Carbohydrate *49 g*; Fat *30 g*; Saturates *11 g*

★★   easy

🕐   15 mins

🕐   1 hr 30 mins

This Italian-style dish is richly flavored with pesto, which is a mixture of basil, olive oil, pine nuts, and Parmesan cheese.

Broiled Chicken *with* Pesto Toasts

SERVES 4

8 part-boned chicken thighs
1 tbsp olive oil for brushing
1²/₃ cups strained tomatoes
½ cup bottled green or red pesto sauce
12 slices French bread
1 cup freshly grated Parmesan cheese
½ cup pine nuts or slivered almonds
salad greens, to serve

1 Arrange the chicken thighs in a single layer in a wide ovenproof dish and brush lightly with olive oil. Cook under a preheated hot broiler for about 15 minutes, turning occasionally, until golden brown.

2 Insert the point of a sharp knife into the thickest part of the meat to make sure there is no trace of pink in the juices.

3 Pour off any excess fat. Warm the strained tomatoes and half the pesto sauce in a small pan over a low heat and pour over the chicken. Cook under the preheated hot broiler for a few more minutes, turning until the chicken is coated.

4 Meanwhile, spread the remaining pesto sauce onto the slices of bread. Arrange the bread over the chicken and sprinkle with the Parmesan cheese. Sprinkle the pine nuts over the cheese. Cook under the preheated hot broiler for 2–3 minutes, or until browned and bubbling. Serve with salad greens.

NUTRITION
Calories *787*; Sugars *6 g*; Protein *45 g*;
Carbohydrate *70 g*; Fat *38 g*; Saturates *9 g*

⭐⭐   easy
🕐   10 mins
🕐   25 mins

 COOK'S TIP

Leaving the skin on means the chicken will have a higher fat content, but many people like the rich taste and crispy skin, especially when it is blackened by the broiler. The skin also keeps in the cooking juices.

This is a popular Italian classic in which browned chicken quarters are cooked in a tomato and bell pepper sauce.

Chicken Cacciatora

1 Rinse the chicken pieces under cold running water and pat dry with paper towels. Mix the flour and salt and pepper to taste on a plate, then lightly dust the chicken pieces with the seasoned flour.

2 Heat the olive oil in a large skillet over a medium heat. Add the chicken and cook until browned all over. Remove from the skillet and set aside.

3 Drain off all but 2 tablespoons of the fat in the skillet. Add the wine and stir for a few minutes. Then add the bell peppers, carrots, celery, and garlic. Season to taste with salt and pepper and let simmer for about 15 minutes.

4 Add the chopped tomatoes to the skillet. Cover and let simmer for about 30 minutes, stirring frequently, until the chicken is cooked through.

5 Transfer the chicken and sauce to 4 large, warmed serving plates and serve.

SERVES 4

1 roasting chicken, about 3 lb 5 oz/1.5 kg, cut into 6–8 serving pieces
1 cup all-purpose flour
3 tbsp olive oil
2/3 cup dry white wine
1 green bell pepper, seeded and sliced
1 red bell pepper, seeded and sliced
1 carrot, chopped finely
1 celery stalk, chopped finely
1 garlic clove, ground
200 g/7 oz canned chopped tomatoes
salt and pepper

NUTRITION
Calories 397; Sugars 4 g; Protein 37 g;
Carbohydrate 22 g; Fat 17 g; Saturates 4 g

 easy

 20 mins

🕐 1 hr

Chicken pieces are cooked in a succulent lemon and mild mustard sauce, then coated in poppy seeds and served on a bed of fresh pasta shells.

Lemon Chicken Conchiglie

SERVES 4

8 chicken pieces, about 4 oz/115 g each
4 tbsp butter, melted
4 tbsp mild mustard (see Cook's Tip)
2 tbsp lemon juice
1 tbsp brown sugar
1 tsp paprika
3 tbsp poppy seeds
3½ cups fresh pasta shells
1 tbsp olive oil
salt and pepper

1 Arrange the chicken pieces, smooth-side down, in a single layer in a large ovenproof dish.

2 Mix the butter, mustard, lemon juice, sugar, and paprika together in a bowl and season to taste with salt and pepper. Brush half the mixture over the upper surfaces of the chicken pieces and bake in a preheated oven at 400°F/200°C, for 15 minutes.

3 Remove the dish from the oven and carefully turn the chicken pieces over with tongs. Coat the upper surfaces of the chicken with the remaining mustard mixture, sprinkle the chicken pieces with poppy seeds, and return to the oven for an additional 15 minutes.

4 Meanwhile, bring a large pan of lightly salted water to a boil over a medium heat. Add the pasta shells and olive oil and cook for 8–10 minutes, or until just done.

5 Drain the pasta thoroughly and arrange in a warmed serving dish. Top with the chicken, then pour over the sauce and serve immediately.

NUTRITION
Calories 652; Sugars 5 g; Protein 51 g; Carbohydrate 46 g; Fat 31 g; Saturates 12 g

easy
10 mins
35 mins

 COOK'S TIP

Dijon is the type of mustard most often used in cooking, as it has a clean and only mildly spicy flavor. German mustard has a sweet-sour taste, with Bavarian mustard being slightly sweeter. American mustard is mild and sweet.

Napoleon's chef was ordered to cook a sumptuous meal on the eve of the battle of Marengo. He gathered everything possible to make a feast, and this was the result.

Chicken Marengo

1 Using a sharp knife, remove the bone from each of the chicken pieces.

2 Heat the 1 tablespoon of the olive oil in a large skillet over a medium heat. Add the chicken pieces and cook for 4–5 minutes, turning occasionally, or until browned all over.

3 Add the strained tomatoes, wine, and mixed herbs to the skillet. Bring to a boil over a medium heat, then let simmer for about 30 minutes, or until the chicken is tender and the juices run clear when the point of a sharp knife is inserted into the thickest part of the meat. Keep warm.

4 Mix the melted butter and ground garlic together in a small bowl. Lightly toast the slices of bread under a preheated hot broiler and brush with the garlic butter. Keep warm.

5 Add the remaining olive oil to a separate skillet over a low heat. Add the mushrooms and cook for 2–3 minutes, or until just brown.

6 Add the olives and sugar to the chicken and cook until warmed through.

7 Transfer the chicken and sauce to 4 warmed serving plates. Garnish with basil leaves and serve with the toast and cooked mushrooms.

SERVES 4

8 chicken pieces
1 tbsp olive oil
1 cup strained tomatoes
3/4 cup white wine
2 tsp dried mixed herbs
4 tbsp butter, melted
2 garlic cloves, ground
8 slices white bread
1½ cups sliced mixed mushrooms (such as white, oyster, and cépes)
16–18 pitted black olives, chopped
1 tsp sugar
fresh basil, to garnish

NUTRITION
Calories 521; Sugars 6 g; Protein 47 g;
Carbohydrate 34 g; Fat 19 g; Saturates 8 g

⭐⭐⭐ moderate

🕐 20 mins

🕐 50 mins

A raspberry and honey sauce superbly counterbalances the richness of the duck.

Duck *with* Raspberry Sauce

S E R V E S 4

4 boneless breasts of duck, about
　　10 oz/285 g each
2 tbsp butter
⅜ cup finely chopped carrots
4 tbsp finely chopped shallots
1 tbsp lemon juice
⅝ cup chicken bouillon
4 tbsp honey
¾ cup fresh or thawed frozen raspberries
¼ cup all-purpose flour
1 tbsp Worcestershire sauce
14 oz/400 g fresh linguine
1 tbsp olive oil
salt and pepper

to garnish
fresh raspberries
1 fresh Italian parsley sprig

N U T R I T I O N
Calories *686*; Sugars *15 g*; Protein *62 g*;
Carbohydrate *70 g*; Fat *20 g*; Saturates *7 g*

⭐⭐　　　　easy
🕐　　　　　15 mins
🕐　　　　　25 mins

1 Trim and score the duck breasts with a sharp knife and season to taste with salt and pepper. Melt the butter in a skillet over a medium heat. Add the duck breasts and cook until lightly colored all over.

2 Add the carrots, shallots, lemon juice, and half the chicken bouillon, then let simmer over a low heat for 1 minute. Stir in half the honey and half the raspberries. Sprinkle over half the flour and cook, stirring constantly, for about 3 minutes. Season with pepper and add the Worcestershire sauce.

3 Stir in the remaining bouillon and cook for 1 minute. Stir in the remaining honey and remaining raspberries, then sprinkle over the remaining flour. Cook for an additional 3 minutes.

4 Remove the duck breasts from the skillet and keep warm. Let the sauce continue to simmer over a very low heat.

5 Meanwhile, bring a large pan of lightly salted water to a boil over a medium heat. Add the pasta and olive oil and cook for 8–10 minutes, or until just done. Drain thoroughly and transfer to 4 warmed serving plates.

6 Slice the duck breast lengthwise into ¼-inch/5-mm thick pieces. Pour a little sauce over the pasta and arrange the sliced duck in a fan shape on top of it. Garnish with raspberries and Italian parsley sprigs and serve.

Partridge has a more delicate flavor than many game birds and this subtle sauce complements it perfectly.

Lime Partridge *with* Pesto

1 Make the pesto sauce (see page 128) and set aside until required.

2 Arrange the partridge pieces, smooth-side down, in a single layer in a large, ovenproof dish. Mix the butter, Dijon mustard, lime juice, and brown sugar together in a bowl. Season to taste with salt and pepper. Brush half of this mixture over the uppermost surfaces of the partridge pieces and bake in a preheated oven at 400°F/200°C, for 15 minutes.

3 Remove the dish from the oven and coat the partridge pieces with half of the pesto sauce. Return to the oven and bake for an additional 12 minutes.

4 Remove the dish from the oven and carefully turn the partridge pieces over and coat the top with the remaining mustard mixture. Return to the oven and bake for an additional 10 minutes.

5 Meanwhile, bring a large pan of lightly salted water to a boil over a medium heat. Add the pasta and cook for about 10 minutes, or until just done. Drain thoroughly and transfer to a large serving dish. Toss the pasta with the remaining pesto sauce and the Parmesan cheese.

6 Serve the partridge with the pasta and pour over the cooking juices.

SERVES 4

6 tbsp Pesto Sauce (see page 128)
8 partridge pieces, about 4 oz/115 g each
4 tbsp butter, melted
4 tbsp Dijon mustard
2 tbsp lime juice
1 tbsp brown sugar
1 lb/450 g dried rigatoni
1 tbsp olive oil
1⅓ cups freshly grated Parmesan cheese
salt and pepper

NUTRITION
Calories *895*; Sugars *5 g*; Protein *79 g*;
Carbohydrate *45 g*; Fat *45 g*; Saturates *18 g*

✪✪✪✪ challenging

🕐 15 mins

🕐 40 mins

Pasta *and* Rice

Pasta and rice are quick and easy to cook and, when combined with a variety of ingredients, can produce an enormous variety of dishes. To cook pasta, bring a pan of lightly salted water to a boil over a medium heat. Add the pasta and 1 teaspoon of olive oil, if you wish. Do not cover, but bring the water to a rolling boil. When the pasta is tender, drain and toss with butter, olive oil, or sauce. As a rough guide, fresh unfilled pasta will take 3 minutes and filled fresh pasta 10 minutes to cook, while dried pasta will take about 10–15 minutes.

To cook a good quality rice like basmati, soak it for about 20–30 minutes to prevent the grains from sticking to each other. Add it to gently boiling, lightly salted water, stir once and cook until tender, but still firm to the bite. This will take 20 minutes.

The original recipe takes about 4 hours to cook and should be left overnight to allow the flavors to mingle. This version is much quicker.

Spaghetti Bolognese

SERVES 4

1 tbsp olive oil
1 onion, chopped finely
2 garlic cloves, chopped
1 carrot, chopped
1 celery stalk, chopped
½ cup pancetta or lean bacon, diced
12 oz/350 g lean ground beef
2 cups chopped tomatoes
2 tsp dried oregano
scant ½ cup red wine
2 tbsp tomato paste
salt and pepper
1½ lb/675 g fresh spaghetti or 350 g/12 oz dried spaghetti
freshly grated Parmesan cheese, to serve (optional)

1 Heat the olive oil in a large skillet over a medium heat. Add the onion and cook for 3 minutes.

2 Add the garlic, carrot, celery, and pancetta or bacon and sauté over a fairly high heat for 3–4 minutes, or until just starting to brown.

3 Add the beef and cook over a high heat for an additional 3 minutes, or until all of the meat is browned.

4 Stir in the tomatoes, oregano, and red wine and bring to a boil over a medium heat. Reduce the heat and let simmer for about 45 minutes.

5 Stir in the tomato paste and season to taste with salt and pepper.

6 Bring a large pan of lightly salted water to a boil over a medium heat. Add the pasta and cook for 8–10 minutes, or until just done, then drain the pasta thoroughly.

7 Transfer the pasta to a large serving plate and pour over the bolognese sauce. Toss to mix well and serve with Parmesan cheese, if you wish.

NUTRITION

Calories 591; Sugars 7 g; Protein 29 g;
Carbohydrate 640 g; Fat 24 g; Saturates 9 g

easy

20 mins

1 hr 5 mins

 COOK'S TIP

Try adding ¼ cup dried porcini, soaked for 20 minutes in 2 tablespoons of warm water, to the bolognese sauce in step 4, if you wish.

Based on a traditional family favorite, this pasta bake has plenty of flavor. Serve with a crisp salad for a quick, tasty supper.

Three-Cheese Macaroni

1 Make the Béchamel sauce (see page 14), transfer it to a bowl, and cover with plastic wrap to prevent a skin forming on the surface of the sauce. Set the sauce aside.

2 Bring a large pan of lightly salted water to a boil over a medium heat. Add the macaroni and cook for 8–10 minutes, or until just done. Drain thoroughly and place in a lightly greased ovenproof dish.

3 Stir the beaten egg, cheddar cheese, mustard, and chives into the Béchamel sauce, then season to taste with salt and pepper.

4 Spoon the sauce over the macaroni, making sure it is well covered. Arrange the sliced tomatoes in a layer over the top.

5 Sprinkle the brick and blue cheeses, and the sunflower seeds evenly over the pasta bake. Put the dish on a cookie sheet and bake in a preheated oven at 375°F/190°C, for 25–30 minutes, or until the topping is bubbling and golden.

6 Garnish the pasta bake with snipped chives and serve immediately on 4 large, warmed plates.

SERVES 4

2½ cups Béchamel Sauce (see page 14)
2 cups dried macaroni
1 egg, beaten
1 cup freshly grated sharp Cheddar cheese
1 tbsp whole-grain mustard
2 tbsp snipped fresh chives
4 tomatoes, sliced
1 cup freshly grated brick cheese
½ cup freshly grated blue cheese
2 tbsp sunflower seeds
salt and pepper
snipped fresh chives, to garnish

NUTRITION
Calories *672*; Sugars *10 g*; Protein *31 g*;
Carbohydrate *40 g*; Fat *44 g*; Saturates *23 g*

 moderate

 30 mins

45 mins

These vegetable crêpes can be filled with your favorite vegetables—try shredded parsnips with a tablespoon of mustard.

Macaroni *and* Corn Pancakes

SERVES 4

2 corn ears
4 tbsp butter
4 oz/115 g red bell peppers, seeded and finely diced
2½ cups dried short-cut macaroni
⅔ cup heavy cream
¼ cup all-purpose flour
4 egg yolks
4 tbsp olive oil
salt and pepper

to serve
oyster mushrooms
sautéed leeks

NUTRITION
Calories 702; Sugars 4 g; Protein 13 g; Carbohydrate 55 g; Fat 50 g; Saturates 23 g

★★★ moderate

🕐. 15 mins

🕐 40 mins

1 Bring a large pan of water to a boil over a medium heat. Add the corn ears, and cook for about 8 minutes. Drain thoroughly and refresh under cold running water for 3 minutes. Carefully cut away the kernels onto paper towels and let dry.

2 Melt 2 tablespoons of the butter in a skillet over a low heat. Add the bell peppers and cook for 4 minutes. Drain and pat dry on paper towels.

3 Bring a large pan of lightly salted water to a boil over a medium heat. Add the macaroni and cook for about 12 minutes, or until just done. Drain thoroughly and let cool in cold water until required.

4 Beat the cream with the flour, a pinch of salt, and the egg yolks in a bowl until smooth. Add the corn kernels and bell peppers. Drain the macaroni and then toss into the corn mixture. Season with pepper to taste.

5 Heat the remaining butter with the olive oil in a large skillet over a medium heat. Drop spoonfuls of the mixture into the skillet and press down until the mixture forms crêpes. Cook until the crêpes are golden on both sides, and all the mixture is used. Drain on paper towels and serve with oyster mushrooms and leeks.

Fresh tomatoes make a delicious Italian-style sauce, which goes particularly well with all types of pasta.

Italian Tomato Sauce *and* Pasta

1 To make the tomato sauce, heat the olive oil in a pan over a low heat. Add the onion and garlic and cook gently until soft.

2 Add the tomatoes, tomato paste, and water. Season to taste with salt and pepper and bring to a boil over a low heat. Cover and let simmer gently for 10 minutes.

3 Meanwhile, bring a large pan of lightly salted water to a boil over a medium heat. Add the pasta and cook for 8–10 minutes, or until just done. Drain thoroughly and transfer to 4 warmed serving dishes.

4 Heat the bacon gently in a skillet over a low heat until the fat runs, then add the mushrooms and cook for 3–4 minutes. Drain off any excess oil.

5 Add the bacon and mushrooms to the tomato mixture together with the chopped parsley or cilantro and sour cream (if using). Reheat gently and serve immediately with the pasta.

SERVES 4

1 tbsp olive oil
1 small onion, chopped finely
1–2 garlic cloves, minced
4 tomatoes, peeled and chopped
2 tsp tomato paste
2 tbsp water
3–4 cups dried pasta shapes
¾ cup lean bacon, rinded and diced
½ cup sliced mushrooms
1 tbsp chopped fresh parsley or
    1 tsp chopped fresh cilantro
2 tbsp sour cream (optional)
salt and pepper

NUTRITION
Calories *304*; Sugars *8 g*; Protein *15 g*;
Carbohydrate *31 g*; Fat *14 g*; Saturates *5 g*

⭐ very easy

🕐 10 mins

🕐 25 mins

The different shapes and textures of the vegetables make a mouthwatering presentation in this light and summery dish.

Broccoli *and* Asparagus Gemelli

SERVES 4

2 cups dried gemelli or other pasta shapes
1 head broccoli, cut into flowerets
2 zucchini, sliced
8 oz/225 g asparagus spears, halved
1½ cups snow peas
1 cup frozen peas
2 tbsp butter
3 tbsp vegetable bouillon
4 tbsp heavy cream
freshly grated nutmeg
2 tbsp chopped fresh parsley
2 tbsp freshly grated Parmesan cheese
salt and pepper

NUTRITION
Calories 517; Sugars 5 g; Protein 17 g;
Carbohydrate 42 g; Fat 32 g; Saturates 18 g

easy

10 mins

25 mins

1 Bring a large pan of lightly salted water to a boil over a medium heat. Add the pasta and cook for about 8–10 minutes, or until just done. Drain thoroughly and return to the pan, cover, and keep warm.

2 Steam the broccoli, zucchini, asparagus spears, and snow peas over a pan of boiling salted water until they are just starting to soften. Remove from the heat and refresh in cold water. Drain and set aside.

3 Bring a small pan of lightly salted water to a boil over a medium heat. Add the frozen peas and cook for 3 minutes. Drain the peas and refresh in cold water, then drain again. Set aside with the other vegetables.

4 Heat the butter and vegetable bouillon in a pan over a medium heat. Add all of the vegetables, and set aside a few of the asparagus spears. Toss carefully with a wooden spoon until they have heated through, taking care not to break them up.

5 Stir in the cream and heat through without bringing to a boil. Season to taste with salt, pepper, and nutmeg.

6 Transfer the pasta to a warmed serving dish and stir in the chopped parsley. Spoon over the vegetable sauce and sprinkle over the Parmesan cheese. Arrange the reserved asparagus spears in a pattern on the top and serve.

Broccoli coated in a garlic-flavored cream sauce, served on fresh herb tagliatelle. Try sprinkling with toasted pine nuts to add an extra crunch.

Pasta with Garlic *and* Broccoli

1 Cut the broccoli into even-size flowerets. Bring a pan of lightly salted water to a boil over a medium heat. Add the broccoli, bring back to a boil and cook for 3 minutes, then drain thoroughly.

2 Place the soft cheese in a pan and heat over a low heat, stirring constantly, until melted. Add the milk and stir until well blended.

3 Add the broccoli to the cheese mixture and stir until the broccoli is coated.

4 Meanwhile, bring a large pan of lightly salted water to a boil over a medium heat. Add the pasta and cook for 3–4 minutes, or until just done.

5 Drain the pasta thoroughly and transfer to 4 warmed serving plates. Spoon the broccoli and cheese sauce on top. Sprinkle with the Parmesan cheese, garnish with snipped chives and serve immediately.

SERVES 4

1 lb 2 oz/500 g broccoli
1⅓ cups garlic and herb cream cheese
4 tbsp milk
12 oz/350 g fresh herb tagliatelle
⅓ cup freshly grated Parmesan cheese
salt
snipped fresh chives, to garnish

NUTRITION
Calories *424*; Sugars *3.5 g*; Protein *15 g*; Carbohydrate *39 g*; Fat *7.7 g*; Saturates *18 g*

⭐⭐   easy

🕐   10 mins

🕐   15 mins

 COOK'S TIP

A herb flavored pasta goes particularly well with the broccoli sauce, but failing this, a tagliatelle verde or "paglia e fieno" (literally "straw and hay"—thin green and yellow noodles) will fit the bill.

A satisfying winter dish, this pasta and bean casserole with a crunchy topping is a slow-cooked, one-pot meal.

Casseroled Beans *and* Penne

SERVES 4

1¼ cups dried navy beans, soaked overnight and drained
2 cups dried penne
3½ cups vegetable bouillon
5 tbsp olive oil
2 large onions, sliced
2 garlic cloves, chopped
2 bay leaves
1 tsp dried oregano
1 tsp dried thyme
5 tbsp red wine
2 tbsp tomato paste
2 celery stalks, sliced
1 fennel bulb, sliced
1⅝ cups sliced mushrooms
8 oz/225 g tomatoes, sliced
1 tsp dark brown sugar
4 tbsp dry white bread crumbs
salt and pepper
salad greens, to serve

NUTRITION
Calories *323*; Sugars *5 g*; Protein *13 g*; Carbohydrate *41 g*; Fat *12 g*; Saturates *2 g*

moderate

25 mins

3 hrs 30 mins

1 Place the navy beans in a large pan and pour over enough cold water to cover. Bring to a boil over a high heat and boil vigorously for 20 minutes. Drain, set aside, and keep warm.

2 Bring a large pan of lightly salted water to a boil over a medium heat. Add the pasta and cook for about 3 minutes. Drain thoroughly, then set aside and keep warm.

3 Place the beans in a large, ovenproof casserole. Add the vegetable bouillon and stir in the olive oil, onions, garlic, bay leaves, oregano, thyme, wine, and tomato paste. Bring to a boil over a medium heat, then cover and cook in a preheated oven at 350°F/180°C, for 2 hours.

4 Add the pasta, celery, fennel, mushrooms, and tomatoes to the casserole and season to taste with salt and pepper. Stir in the brown sugar and sprinkle over the bread crumbs. Cover and cook in the oven for 1 additional hour.

5 Remove the casserole from the oven and transfer to 4 warmed serving plates and serve with salad greens.

A Mediterranean mixture of red bell peppers, garlic, and zucchini, cooked in olive oil and tossed with pasta spirals.

Pasta *and* Vegetable Sauce

1 Heat the olive oil in a heavy-based pan or ovenproof casserole over a medium heat. Add the onion and garlic and cook, stirring occasionally, until the onion has softened. Add the bell peppers and zucchini and cook, stirring occasionally, for 5 minutes.

2 Add the tomatoes, sun-dried tomato paste, and basil, and season to taste with salt and pepper. Cover and cook for an additional 5 minutes.

3 Meanwhile, bring a large pan of lightly salted water to a boil over a medium heat. Add the pasta and cook for 3 minutes, or until just done. Drain thoroughly and add to the vegetable mixture. Toss gently to mix well.

4 Place the mixture in a shallow ovenproof dish and sprinkle with the cheese.

5 Cook under a preheated hot broiler for 5 minutes, or until the cheese is golden brown and bubbling. Transfer to 4 warmed serving plates, garnish with basil sprigs and serve.

SERVES 4

3 tbsp olive oil
1 onion, sliced
2 garlic cloves, chopped
3 red bell peppers, seeded and cut into strips
3 zucchini, sliced
14 oz/400 g canned chopped tomatoes
3 tbsp sun-dried tomato paste
2 tbsp chopped fresh basil
2 cups fresh fusilli
1 cup freshly grated Swiss cheese
salt and pepper
fresh basil sprigs, to garnish

NUTRITION
Calories *341*; Sugars *8 g*; Protein *13 g*;
Carbohydrate *30 g*; Fat *20 g*; Saturates *8 g*

 very easy

15 mins

20 mins

🎩 **COOK'S TIP**

Be careful not to overcook fresh pasta—it should be *al dente* (retaining some "bite"). It takes only a few minutes to cook as it is still full of moisture.

Delicious stirred into pasta, soups, and salad dressings, pesto is available in most supermarkets, but making your own gives a much fresher, fuller flavor.

Pasta *with* Classic Pesto Sauce

SERVES 4

about 40 fresh basil leaves, washed and dried
3 garlic cloves, minced
¼ cup pine nuts
½ cup finely grated Parmesan cheese
2–3 tbsp extra virgin olive oil
salt and pepper
1½ lb/675 g fresh pasta or 12 oz/350 g dried pasta

1 Rinse the basil leaves in cold water and pat them dry on paper towels.

2 Place the basil leaves, garlic, pine nuts, and Parmesan cheese into a food processor and blend for about 30 seconds, or until smooth. Alternatively, pound the ingredients by hand, using a mortar and pestle.

3 If you are using a food processor, keep the motor running and slowly add the olive oil. Alternatively, add the olive oil drop by drop while stirring briskly. Season to taste with salt and pepper.

4 Meanwhile, bring a large pan of lightly salted water to a boil over a medium heat. Add the pasta and cook for until just done. Drain thoroughly.

5 Transfer the pasta to 4 warmed serving plates and serve with the pesto. Toss to mix well and serve immediately.

NUTRITION
Calories 155; Sugars 2.5 g; Protein 5.2 g;
Carbohydrate 0.5 g; Fat 14.6 g; Saturates 7 g

very easy

15 mins

10 mins

 COOK'S TIP

You can store pesto in the refrigerator for about 4 weeks. Cover the surface of the pesto with olive oil before sealing the container or bottle, to prevent the basil from oxidizing and turning black.

This easy and satisfying Roman dish originated as a cheap meal for poor people, but has now become a favorite in restaurants and trattorias.

Garlic Spaghetti

1 Set aside 1 teaspoon of the olive oil and heat the remainder in a medium pan over a low heat. Add the garlic and a pinch of salt and cook, stirring constantly, until golden brown, then remove the pan from the heat. Do not let the garlic burn as this will taint the flavor of the oil. (If it does burn, you will have to start all over again!)

2 Meanwhile, bring a large pan of lightly salted water to a boil over a medium heat. Add the pasta and remaining olive oil and cook for about 2–3 minutes, or until done. Drain thoroughly and return to the pan.

3 Add the olive oil and garlic mixture to the pasta and toss to coat thoroughly. Season with pepper to taste, add the chopped parsley and toss well to coat.

4 Transfer the pasta to 4 warmed serving dishes and serve immediately.

SERVES 4

½ cup olive oil
3 garlic cloves, minced
1 lb/450 g fresh spaghetti
3 tbsp coarsely chopped fresh parsley
salt and pepper

NUTRITION
Calories 477; Sugars 1.8 g; Protein 0.6 g;
Carbohydrate 37 g; Fat 40 g; Saturates 3 g

easy

10 mins

10 mins

COOK'S TIP

Oils produced by different countries—mainly Italy, Spain, and Greece—have their own characteristic flavors. Some produce an oil which has a hot, peppery taste, while others have a "green" flavor.

This is a simple, clean-tasting dish of green vegetables, bean curd, and pasta, lightly tossed in olive oil.

Vegetables *and* Bean Curd

SERVES 4

1 cup asparagus
1 cup snow peas
2 cups green beans
1 leek
2²⁄₃ cups shelled small fava beans
2¹⁄₂ cups dried fusilli
2 tbsp olive oil
2 tbsp butter
1 garlic clove, minced
8 oz/225 g bean curd, cut into 1-inch/
   2.5-cm cubes (drained weight)
5 tbsp pitted green olives in brine, drained
salt and pepper
freshly grated Parmesan cheese, to serve

NUTRITION
Calories *400*; Sugars *5 g*; Protein *19 g*;
Carbohydrate *46 g*; Fat *17 g*; Saturates *5 g*

★★   easy

            25 mins

            20 mins

1 Cut the asparagus into 2-inch/5-cm lengths. Thinly slice the snow peas diagonally and slice the green beans into 1-inch/2.5-cm pieces. Thinly slice the leek.

2 Bring a large pan of water to a boil over a medium heat. Add the asparagus, green beans, and fava beans. Bring the water back to a boil and cook for about 4 minutes. Drain thoroughly, rinse in cold water and drain again, then set aside.

3 Bring a large pan of lightly salted water to a boil over a medium heat. Add the pasta and cook for 8–10 minutes, or until just done. Drain thoroughly. Toss in 1 tablespoon of the olive oil and season to taste with salt and pepper.

4 Meanwhile, heat the remaining olive oil and butter in a preheated wok or large skillet over a low heat. Add the leek, garlic, and bean curd and gently cook for 1–2 minutes, or until the vegetables have just softened.

5 Stir in the snow peas and cook for 1 additional minute.

6 Add the blanched vegetables and olives to the wok or skillet and heat through for 1 minute. Carefully stir in the pasta and adjust the seasoning, if necessary. Cook for 1 minute and pile into a warmed serving dish. Serve immediately with Parmesan cheese.

A deliciously fresh and slightly spicy tomato sauce, which is excellent for lunch or a light supper.

Chile Tagliatelle

1 Melt the butter in a large pan over a medium heat. Add the onion and garlic and cook for 3–4 minutes, or until softened.

2 Add the chiles to the pan and cook for about 2 minutes.

3 Add the tomatoes and bouillon, then reduce the heat to low and let simmer for 10 minutes, stirring constantly.

4 Pour the sauce into a food processor and process for about 1 minute, or until smooth. Alternatively, rub the sauce through a strainer.

5 Return the sauce to the pan and add the tomato paste, sugar, and salt and pepper to taste. Gently reheat over a low heat, until piping hot.

6 Bring a large pan of lightly salted water to a boil over a medium heat. Add the pasta and cook until just done. Drain thoroughly and transfer to 4 large, warmed serving plates and serve immediately with the sauce.

SERVES 4

3 tbsp butter
1 onion, chopped finely
1 garlic clove, minced
2 small red chiles, seeded and diced
1 lb/450 g fresh tomatoes, peeled, seeded, and diced
¾ cup vegetable bouillon
2 tbsp tomato paste
1 tsp sugar
1 ½ lb/675 g fresh green and white tagliatelle, or 12 oz/350 g dried tagliatelle
salt and pepper

NUTRITION
Calories *306*; Sugars *7 g*; Protein *8 g*; Carbohydrate *45 g*; Fat *12 g*; Saturates *7 g*

⭐⭐ easy
🕐 15 mins
🕐 35 mins

 COOK'S TIP

Try topping your pasta dish with ½ cup pancetta or unsmoked bacon, diced and dry-fried for 5 minutes, or until crispy.

These delicious individual pasta molds are served with a tasty tomato sauce, flavored with bay leaf.

Pasta *and* Cheese Molds

SERVES 4

1 tbsp butter, softened
½ cup dried white bread crumbs
6 oz/175 g tricolor spaghetti
1¼ cups Béchamel Sauce (see page 14)
1 egg yolk
1 cup freshly grated Swiss cheese
salt and pepper
fresh Italian parsley sprigs, to garnish

tomato sauce
2 tsp olive oil
1 onion, chopped finely
1 bay leaf
⅔ cup dry white wine
⅔ cup strained tomatoes
1 tbsp tomato paste

NUTRITION
Calories *517*; Sugars *8 g*; Protein *19 g*;
Carbohydrate *47 g*; Fat *27 g*; Saturates *13 g*

⭐⭐⭐   moderate

🕐   45 mins

🕐   50 mins

1 Grease four ¾-cup molds or ramekins with the butter. Evenly coat the insides with half of the bread crumbs.

2 Break the pasta into 2-inch/5-cm lengths. Bring a pan of lightly salted water to a boil over a medium heat. Add the pasta and cook for about 5–6 minutes, or until just done. Drain thoroughly and place in a bowl.

3 Mix the Béchamel sauce (see page 14), egg yolk, and cheese into the cooked pasta, then season to taste with salt and pepper. Pack the mixture carefully into the molds.

4 Sprinkle over the remaining bread crumbs and place the molds on a cookie sheet. Bake in a preheated oven at 425°F/220°C, for 20 minutes, or until golden brown. Let stand for 10 minutes.

5 Meanwhile, to make the sauce, heat the olive oil in a skillet over a low heat. Add the onion and bay leaf and sauté for 2–3 minutes, or until the onion is just softened.

6 Stir in the wine, strained tomatoes, tomato paste, and season to taste. Bring the sauce to a boil and let simmer for 20 minutes, or until thickened. Remove from the heat and discard the bay leaf.

7 Run a spatula around the inside of the molds. Turn out onto 4 serving plates, garnish with parsley sprigs, and serve with the sauce.

This mouthwatering dish would make an excellent light vegetarian lunch for four or a good appetizer for six.

Walnut *and* Olive Pasta

1 Place the bread in a large, shallow dish, pour over the milk, then let soak until the liquid is absorbed.

2 Spread the walnuts out onto a cookie sheet and toast in a preheated oven at 375°F/190°C, for about 5 minutes, or until golden. Let cool.

3 Place the bread, walnuts, garlic, olives, Parmesan cheese, and 6 tablespoons of the olive oil in a food processor and process until a paste forms. Season to taste with salt and pepper, then stir in the cream.

4 Bring a large pan of lightly salted water to a boil over a medium heat. Add the pasta and 1 teaspoon of the remaining olive oil and cook for about 2–3 minutes, or until just done. Drain thoroughly, then toss with the remaining olive oil.

5 Transfer the pasta to warmed serving plates and spoon the olive, garlic, and walnut sauce on top. Sprinkle over the chopped parsley, then serve.

SERVES 4 – 6

2 thick slices whole-wheat bread, crusts removed
1¼ cups milk
2½ cups shelled walnuts
2 garlic cloves, minced
1 cup pitted black olives
⅔ cup freshly grated Parmesan cheese
8 tbsp extra virgin olive oil
⅝ cup heavy cream
1 lb/450 g fresh fettuccine
2–3 tbsp chopped fresh parsley
salt and pepper

NUTRITION
Calories *833*; Sugars *5 g*; Protein *20 g*; Carbohydrate *44 g*; Fat *66 g*; Saturates *15 g*

 easy

15 mins

10 mins

COOK'S TIP

Grated Parmesan cheese quickly loses its pungency and bite. It is better to buy small quantities and grate it yourself. Wrapped in aluminum foil, it will keep in the refrigerator for several months.

This light pasta dish has a delicate flavor ideally suited to a summer lunch.

Spaghetti *with* Ricotta Cheese

SERVES 4

12 oz/350 g dried spaghetti
3 tbsp butter
2 tbsp chopped fresh Italian parsley
1 tbsp pine nuts
salt and pepper
fresh Italian parsley sprigs, to garnish

ricotta cheese sauce
1 cup freshly ground almonds
½ cup ricotta cheese
pinch of freshly grated nutmeg
pinch of ground cinnamon
⅝ cup plain yogurt
½ cup hot chicken bouillon

1 Bring a large pan of lightly salted water to a boil over a medium heat. Add the pasta and cook for 8–10 minutes, or until just done.

2 Drain the pasta thoroughly, return to the pan, and toss with the butter and chopped parsley. Set aside and keep warm.

3 To make the sauce, mix the ground almonds, ricotta cheese, nutmeg, cinnamon, and yogurt together in a small pan over a low heat until it forms a thick paste. Gradually stir in the olive oil. When the oil has been fully incorporated, gradually stir in the hot chicken bouillon, until smooth. Season to taste with salt and pepper.

4 Transfer the pasta to a warmed serving dish, pour over the sauce, and toss together well with 2 forks (see Cook's Tip). Sprinkle over the pine nuts, garnish with the Italian parsley, and serve immediately.

NUTRITION

Calories 701; Sugars 12 g; Protein 17 g; Carbohydrate 73 g; Fat 40 g; Saturates 15 g

easy

5 mins

25 mins

👨‍🍳 COOK'S TIP

Use 2 large forks to toss spaghetti or other long pasta, as this ensures the pasta is thoroughly coated with the sauce. Special spaghetti forks are available from some cookware departments and kitchen stores.

The tasty flavors and delightful textures of artichoke hearts and black olives make a winning combination.

Artichoke *and* Olive Spaghetti

1 Heat 1 tablespoon of the olive oil in a large, heavy-bottomed skillet over a low heat. Add the onion, garlic, lemon juice, and eggplant and cook, stirring occasionally, for 4–5 minutes, or until lightly browned.

2 Pour in the strained tomatoes, season to taste with salt and pepper, then stir in the sugar and tomato paste. Bring to a boil over a medium heat, then reduce the heat and let simmer gently for 20 minutes.

3 Gently stir in the artichoke hearts and olives and cook for 5 minutes.

4 Meanwhile, bring a large pan of lightly salted water to a boil over a medium heat. Add the pasta and cook for 8–10 minutes, or until just done. Drain thoroughly, toss in the remaining olive oil, and season to taste with salt and pepper.

5 Transfer the pasta to 4 warmed serving bowls and top with the vegetable sauce. Garnish with basil sprigs and serve immediately.

SERVES 4

2 tbsp olive oil
1 large red onion, chopped
2 garlic cloves, minced
1 tbsp lemon juice
4 baby eggplant, cut into fourths
2½ cups strained tomatoes
2 tsp superfine sugar
2 tbsp tomato paste
14 oz/400 g canned artichoke hearts, drained and halved
1 cup pitted black olives
12 oz/350 g whole-wheat dried spaghetti
salt and pepper
fresh basil sprigs, to garnish

NUTRITION
Calories *393*; Sugars *11 g*; Protein *14 g*;
Carbohydrate *63 g*; Fat *11 g*; Saturates *2 g*

⭐⭐   easy

🕐   20 mins

     35 mins

This delicious roasted bell pepper and chile sauce is sweet and spicy.

Fusilli Salad *with* Chile

SERVES 4

2 red bell peppers, halved and seeded
1 small fresh red chile
2 garlic cloves
4 tomatoes, halved
⅔ cup chopped almonds
7 tbsp olive oil
1½ lb/675 g fresh pasta or
    12 oz/350 g dried pasta
fresh oregano leaves, to garnish

NUTRITION
Calories *423*; Sugars *5 g*; Protein *9 g*;
Carbohydrate *38 g*; Fat *27 g*; Saturates *4 g*

moderate

25 mins

30 mins

1 Place the bell peppers, skin-side up, on a cookie sheet with the chile, garlic, and tomatoes, skin-side down. Cook under a preheated hot broiler for about 10–15 minutes, or until the skins are charred and blistered. After 8 minutes, turn the tomatoes skin-side up.

2 Place the bell peppers and chile in a plastic bag and let them sweat for about 10 minutes.

3 Remove the skin from the bell peppers, then seed and peel the chile. Using a sharp knife, slice the flesh into strips.

4 Peel the garlic, then peel and seed the tomatoes.

5 Place the almonds on a cookie sheet and cook under the preheated hot broiler for 2–3 minutes, or until golden.

6 Place the bell pepper, chile, garlic, and tomatoes in a food processor and process until a paste forms. Keep the motor running and slowly add the olive oil to form a thick sauce. Alternatively, mash the mixture with a fork and beat in the olive oil, drop by drop.

7 Stir the toasted almonds into the mixture.

8 Place the sauce in a pan and warm until it is heated through.

9 Bring a large pan of lightly salted water to a boil over a medium heat. Add the pasta and cook until just done. Drain and transfer to 4 warmed serving dishes. Pour over the sauce. Garnish with oregano and serve.

Simple and inexpensive,
this tasty dish is fairly
quick and easy to prepare,
but looks very impressive.

Pasta *with* Nuts *and* Cheese

1 Sprinkle the pine nuts onto a cookie sheet and cook under a preheated hot broiler, turning occasionally, until lightly browned all over. Set aside.

2 Bring a large pan of lightly salted water to a boil over a medium heat. Add the pasta and cook until just done.

3 Meanwhile, cook the zucchini and broccoli in a small amount of boiling, lightly salted water for about 5 minutes, or until just tender.

4 Place the soft cheese in a pan and heat over a low heat, stirring constantly. Add the milk and stir. Add the basil and mushrooms and cook gently for 2–3 minutes. Stir in the blue cheese and season to taste with salt and pepper.

5 Drain the pasta and vegetables and mix together in a serving dish. Pour the cheese and mushroom sauce over and add the pine nuts. Using 2 forks, toss gently to mix. Garnish with a basil sprig and serve with salad greens.

SERVES 4

½ cup pine nuts
3 cups dried pasta shapes
2 zucchini, sliced
1 cup broccoli, broken into flowerets
1 cup full-fat soft cheese
⅔ cup milk
1 tbsp chopped fresh basil
1 cup sliced white mushrooms
⅔ cup crumbled blue cheese
salt and pepper
1 fresh basil sprig, to garnish
salad greens, to serve

NUTRITION
Calories *531*; Sugars *4 g*; Protein *20 g*;
Carbohydrate *35 g*; Fat *35 g*; Saturates *16 g*

⭐⭐   easy

🕐   10 mins

🕐   30 mins

The pappardelle and vegetables are tossed in a delicious chili and tomato sauce for a quick and economical meal.

Pasta *and* Chili Tomatoes

SERVES 4

10 oz/280 g dried pappardelle
3 tbsp peanut oil
2 garlic cloves, minced
2 shallots, sliced
2¼ cups sliced green beans
8 cherry tomatoes, halved
1 tsp chili flakes
4 tbsp crunchy peanut butter
⅔ cup coconut milk
1 tbsp tomato paste

1 Bring a large pan of lightly salted water to a boil over a medium heat. Add the pasta and cook for 8–10 minutes, or until just done. Drain the pasta thoroughly, set aside and keep warm.

2 Meanwhile, heat the peanut oil in a large, heavy-bottomed skillet or preheated wok over a medium heat. Add the garlic and shallots and cook for 1 minute.

3 Add the green beans and drained pasta to the skillet or wok and cook for 5 minutes. Add the cherry tomatoes and mix well.

4 Mix the chili flakes, peanut butter, coconut milk, and tomato paste together. Pour the chili mixture into the skillet or wok, toss well and heat through.

5 Transfer the pasta to 4 warmed serving dishes and serve immediately.

NUTRITION
Calories *353*; Sugars *7 g*; Protein *10 g*;
Carbohydrate *26 g*; Fat *24 g*; Saturates *4 g*

⭐ very easy

🕐 15 mins

🕐 20 mins

 COOK'S TIP

Add slices of chicken or beef to the recipe and stir-fry with the beans and pasta in step 3 for a more substantial main meal.

The smoked salmon ideally complements the spaghetti to give a very luxurious dish.

Spaghetti *and* Salmon Sauce

1 Bring a large pan of lightly salted water to a boil over a medium heat. Add the pasta and cook for 8–10 minutes, or until just done. Drain thoroughly, then return to the pan and sprinkle over the olive oil. Cover the pan and shake well. Set aside and keep warm until required.

2 To make the sauce, heat the cream and the whiskey or brandy in separate small pans to simmering point. Do not let them boil.

3 Mix the cream with the whiskey or brandy together in a bowl.

4 Cut the smoked salmon into thin strips and add to the cream mixture. Season to taste with a little pepper and cayenne pepper, then stir in the chopped cilantro or parsley.

5 Transfer the pasta to a warmed serving dish, pour on the sauce, and toss thoroughly with 2 large forks. Sprinkle the crumbled cheese over the pasta and garnish with the cilantro or parsley. Serve immediately.

SERVES   4

1 lb/450 g dried buckwheat spaghetti
2 tbsp olive oil
½ cup feta cheese, crumbled (drained weight)
1 tbsp chopped fresh cilantro or parsley, to garnish

sauce

1¼ cups heavy cream
⅔ cup whiskey or brandy
4 oz/125 g smoked salmon
large pinch of cayenne pepper
2 tbsp chopped fresh cilantro or parsley
salt and pepper

NUTRITION
Calories *782*; Sugars *3 g*; Protein *20 g*;
Carbohydrate *48 g*; Fat *48 g*; Saturates *27 g*

⭐ very easy
 10 mins
 15 mins

Frozen shelled shrimp from the freezer can become the star ingredient in this colorful and tasty dish.

Spaghetti *and* Shellfish

SERVES 4

8 oz/225 g dried short-cut spaghetti
1 tbsp olive oil
1¼ cups chicken bouillon
1 tsp lemon juice
1 small cauliflower, cut into flowerets
2 carrots, sliced thinly
1½ cups snow peas
4 tbsp butter
1 onion, sliced
2 cups thinly sliced zucchini
1 garlic clove, chopped
12 oz/350 g frozen shelled shrimp, thawed
2 tbsp chopped fresh parsley
⅓ cup freshly grated Parmesan cheese
½ tsp paprika
salt and pepper
4 whole shrimp, to garnish (optional)

1 Bring a large pan of lightly salted water to a boil over a medium heat. Add the pasta and cook for 8–10 minutes, or until done. Drain thoroughly, then return to the pan and stir in the olive oil. Cover and keep warm.

2 Bring the bouillon and lemon juice to a boil over a medium heat. Add the cauliflower and carrots and cook for 3–4 minutes until barely tender. Remove with a slotted spoon and set aside. Add the snow peas and cook for 1–2 minutes, or until they start to soften. Remove with a slotted spoon and add to the other vegetables. Set aside the stock for future use.

3 Melt half the butter in a skillet over a medium heat. Add the onion and zucchini and cook for about 3 minutes. Add the garlic and shrimp and cook for an additional 2–3 minutes, or until thoroughly heated through.

4 Stir in the reserved vegetables and heat through. Season to taste with salt and pepper, then stir in the remaining butter.

5 Transfer the pasta to a warmed serving dish. Pour on the sauce and sprinkle with parsley. Using 2 forks, toss well until thoroughly coated. Sprinkle on the Parmesan cheese and paprika, then garnish with the shrimp (if using). Serve.

NUTRITION
Calories *510*; Sugars *38 g*; Protein *33 g*;
Carbohydrate *44 g*; Fat *24 g*; Saturates *11 g*

moderate

35 mins

30 mins

Fresh clams are available from most supermarkets. If you prefer, use canned clams, which are less messy to eat but not so pretty to serve.

Pasta *with* Clams *and* White Wine

1 If you are using fresh clams, scrub them clean and discard any that are already open.

2 Heat the olive oil in a large skillet over a medium heat. Add the garlic and clams and cook for 2 minutes, shaking the skillet to ensure that all the clams are coated in the oil.

3 Add the remaining seafood mixture to the skillet and cook for an additional 2 minutes.

4 Pour the wine and bouillon over the mixed seafood and garlic and bring to a boil over a medium heat. Cover, then reduce the heat and let simmer for 8–10 minutes, or until the shells open. Discard any shells that are still closed.

5 Meanwhile, bring a large pan of lightly salted water to a boil over a medium heat. Add the pasta and cook until just done. Drain thoroughly.

6 Stir the tarragon into the sauce and season to taste with salt and pepper.

7 Transfer the pasta to a serving plate and pour over the sauce. Serve.

SERVES 4

1½ lb/675 g fresh clams or 10 oz/285 g canned clams, drained

2 tbsp olive oil

2 garlic cloves, chopped finely

1 lb/450 g mixed seafood, such as shrimp, squid, and mussels, thawed if frozen

⅔ cup white wine

⅔ cup fish bouillon

1½ lb/675 g fresh pasta or 12 oz/350 g dried pasta

2 tbsp chopped fresh tarragon

salt and pepper

NUTRITION
Calories *410*; Sugars *1 g*; Protein *39 g*; Carbohydrate *39 g*; Fat *9 g*; Saturates *1 g*

easy

20 mins

20 mins

🍴 **COOK'S TIP**

Red clam sauce can be made by adding 8 tablespoons of strained tomatoes to the sauce along with the bouillon in step 4. Follow the same cooking method.

The creamy, nutty flavor of squash complements the *al dente* texture of the pasta. This recipe has been adapted for cooking in a microwave oven.

Penne *and* Butternut Squash

SERVES 4

2 tbsp olive oil
1 garlic clove, minced
1 cup fresh white bread crumbs
1 lb/450 g butternut squash, peeled, seeded, and diced
8 tbsp water
1 lb/450 g fresh penne, or other pasta shapes
1 tbsp butter
1 onion, sliced
4 oz/100 g ham, cut into strips
scant 1 cup light cream
½ cup freshly grated cheddar cheese
2 tbsp chopped fresh parsley
salt and pepper

1 Mix the olive oil, garlic, and bread crumbs together and spread out on a large plate. Cook in the microwave on High power for 4–5 minutes, stirring every minute, until crisp and starting to brown. Remove and set aside.

2 Place the squash in a large bowl with half the water. Cover and cook on High power for 8–9 minutes, stirring occasionally. Let stand for 2 minutes.

3 Place the pasta in a large bowl, add a little salt, and pour over enough boiling water to cover by 1 inch/2.5 cm. Cover and cook on High power for 5 minutes, stirring once, until the pasta is just done. Let stand, covered, for 1 minute before draining.

4 Place the butter and onion in a large bowl. Cover and cook on High power for 3 minutes.

5 Using a fork, coarsely mash the squash. Add to the onion with the pasta, ham, cream, cheese, parsley, and remaining water. Season generously and mix well. Cover and cook on High power for 4 minutes until heated through.

6 Transfer the pasta to a large, warmed serving dish, sprinkle with the crisp garlic crumbs, and serve.

NUTRITION
Calories *499*; Sugars *4 g*; Protein *20 g*;
Carbohydrate *49 g*; Fat *26 g*; Saturates *13 g*

easy

15 mins

30 mins

These large pasta nests look impressive filled with broiled mixed vegetables and they taste delicious.

Vegetable Pasta Nests

1 Bring a large pan of lightly salted water to a boil over a medium heat. Add the pasta and cook for about 8–10 minutes, or until just done. Drain thoroughly and set aside until required.

2 Place the eggplant, zucchini, and bell pepper on a cookie sheet.

3 Mix the oil and garlic together in a small bowl and pour over the vegetables, tossing to coat thoroughly.

4 Cook the vegetables under a preheated hot broiler for 10 minutes, turning occasionally, until tender and lightly charred. Set aside and keep warm.

5 Lightly grease 4 large, shallow muffin pans with a little butter and divide the pasta among them. Using 2 forks, curl the spaghetti to form nests.

6 Brush the pasta nests with melted butter and sprinkle with the bread crumbs. Bake in a preheated oven at 400°F/200°C, for 15 minutes, or until lightly golden. Remove the nests from the pans and transfer to 4 warmed serving plates. Divide the broiled vegetables between the pasta nests, season to taste with salt and pepper, and garnish with parsley sprigs.

SERVES 4

6 oz/175 g dried spaghetti
1 eggplant, halved and sliced
1 zucchini, diced
1 red bell pepper, seeded and diagonally chopped
6 tbsp olive oil
2 garlic cloves, minced
4 tbsp butter, melted, plus extra for greasing
1 tbsp dry white bread crumbs
salt and pepper
4 fresh parsley sprigs, to garnish

NUTRITION
Calories *392*; Sugars *1 g*; Protein *6 g*;
Carbohydrate *32 g*; Fat *28 g*; Saturates *6 g*

⭐⭐⭐   moderate
🕑   25 mins
🕐   40 mins

👨‍🍳 COOK'S TIP

The Italian term *al dente* means 'to the bite' and describes cooked pasta that is not too soft, but still has a 'bite' to it.

A recipe that has both Italian and Greek origins, this dish may be served hot or cold, cut into thick, satisfying squares.

Pasticcio

SERVES 6

3 ½ cups dried fusilli, or other short
    pasta shapes
1 tbsp olive oil
4 tbsp heavy cream
salt and pepper
fresh rosemary sprigs, to garnish

sauce

2 tbsp olive oil, plus extra for brushing
1 onion, sliced thinly
1 red bell pepper, seeded and chopped
2 garlic cloves, chopped
1½ lb/675 g lean ground beef
14 oz/400 g canned chopped tomatoes
½ cup dry white wine
2 tbsp chopped fresh parsley
1¾ oz/50 g canned anchovy fillets, drained

topping

1 ¼ cups plain yogurt
3 eggs
pinch of freshly grated nutmeg
⅔ cup freshly grated Parmesan cheese

NUTRITION

Calories *590*; Sugars *8 g*; Protein *34 g*;
Carbohydrate *23 g*; Fat *39 g*; Saturates *16 g*

easy

35 mins

1 hr 15 mins

1   To make the sauce, heat the olive oil in a large skillet over a medium heat. Add the onion and bell pepper and cook for 3 minutes. Stir in the garlic and cook for 1 minute. Add the beef and cook, stirring frequently, until browned.

2   Add the tomatoes and wine, stir well, and bring to a boil over a medium heat. Let simmer for 20 minutes, or until the sauce is fairly thick. Chop the anchovies and stir into the sauce with the parsley and season to taste with salt and pepper.

3   Bring a large pan of lightly salted water to a boil over a medium heat. Add the pasta and cook for about 8–10 minutes, or until just done. Drain thoroughly, then transfer to a bowl. Stir in the cream and set aside.

4   To make the topping, beat the yogurt and eggs together, then season to taste with nutmeg, salt, and pepper.

5   Brush a large, shallow casserole with olive oil. Spoon in half the pasta mixture and cover with half the meat sauce. Repeat these layers, then spread the topping over the final layer. Sprinkle the Parmesan cheese evenly on top.

6   Bake in a preheated oven at 375°F/ 190°C, for 25 minutes, or until the topping is golden brown and bubbling. Garnish with rosemary sprigs and serve immediately.

These tasty little squares of pasta stuffed with mushrooms and cheese are surprisingly filling. Serve about 3 pieces for an appetizer and up to 9 for a main course.

Cheesy Pasta Squares

1 Using a serrated pasta cutter, cut 2-inch/5-cm squares from the sheets of fresh pasta. To make 36 pasta squares, you will need 72 squares. Once the pasta is cut, cover the squares with plastic wrap to stop them drying out.

2 Heat 3 tablespoons of the butter in a large skillet over a low heat. Add the shallots, 1 minced garlic clove, mushrooms, and celery, and cook for about 4–5 minutes.

3 Remove the skillet from the heat, then stir in the cheese and season to taste with salt and pepper.

4 Spoon ½ teaspoon of the mixture onto the center of 36 pasta squares. Brush the edges of the squares with water and top with the remaining 36 squares. Press the edges together to seal. Let rest for 5 minutes.

5 Bring a large pan of water to a boil over a medium heat. Add the olive oil and cook the pasta squares, in batches, for 2–3 minutes. The squares will rise to the surface when cooked and the pasta should be tender with a slight bite. Remove from the pan with a slotted spoon and drain.

6 Meanwhile, melt the remaining butter in a pan over a low heat. Add the remaining garlic and plenty of pepper and cook for 1–2 minutes.

7 Transfer the pasta squares to 4 serving plates and pour over the garlic butter. Garnish with the romano cheese and serve immediately.

SERVES 4

10 oz/285 g thin sheets of fresh pasta
5 tbsp butter
½ cup finely chopped shallots
3 garlic cloves, minced
½ cup finely chopped mushrooms
½ celery stalk, chopped finely
¼ cup finely grated romano cheese,
　　plus extra to garnish
1 tbsp oil
salt and pepper

NUTRITION
Calories 360; Sugars 1 g; Protein 9 g;
Carbohydrate 36 g; Fat 21 g; Saturates 12 g

 challenging

1 hr 15 mins

25 mins

Spinach ribbon noodles covered with a rich tomato sauce and topped with creamy chicken make a very appetizing dish.

Tagliatelle *and* Chicken Sauce

SERVES 4

Basic Tomato Sauce (see page 14)
1 lb 7 oz/650 g fresh green tagliatelle or 12 oz/350 g dried tagliatelle
salt
fresh basil leaves, to garnish

chicken sauce
4 tbsp sweet butter
14 oz/400 g skinless boneless chicken breast portions, sliced thinly
¾ cup blanched almonds
1¼ cups heavy cream
salt and pepper

1 Make the tomato sauce (see page 14), set aside, and keep warm.

2 To make the chicken sauce, melt the butter in a large skillet over a medium heat. Add the chicken strips and almonds and cook, stirring frequently, for about 5–6 minutes, or until the chicken is cooked through.

3 Meanwhile, pour the cream into a small pan, set over low heat, and bring to a boil. Boil for about 10 minutes until reduced by almost half. Pour the cream over the chicken and almonds, stir well, and season to taste with salt and pepper. Remove the pan from the heat, set aside, and keep warm.

4 Bring a large pan of lightly salted water to a boil over a medium heat. Add the pasta and cook until just done. Fresh tagliatelle will take 2–3 minutes and dried pasta will take 8–10 minutes. Drain thoroughly, then return to the pan, cover, and keep warm.

5 When ready to serve, transfer the pasta to a warmed serving dish and spoon the tomato sauce over it. Spoon the chicken and cream into the center, sprinkle with the basil leaves, and serve.

NUTRITION
Calories *853*; Sugars *6 g*; Protein *32 g*; Carbohydrate *23 g*; Fat *71 g*; Saturates *34 g*

⭐⭐ easy

🕑 30 mins

🕐 25 mins

If preferred, long-grain rice can be used instead of risotto rice, but it won't give you the traditional, deliciously creamy texture that is so typical of Italian risottos.

Golden Chicken Risotto

1 Heat the corn oil and butter in a large pan over a medium-low heat. Add the leek and yellow bell pepper and sauté for 1 minute, then stir in the chicken and cook, stirring constantly, until golden brown.

2 Stir in the rice and cook for 2–3 minutes. Add the saffron strands, and season to taste with salt and pepper.

3 Add the chicken bouillon, a little at a time and cook over a low heat, stirring constantly, for about 20 minutes, or until the rice is tender and most of the liquid has been absorbed. Do not let the risotto dry out—add more bouillon, if necessary.

4 Stir in the corn, peanuts, and the Parmesan cheese, then adjust the seasoning to taste, if necessary. Transfer to 4 warmed serving plates and serve immediately.

SERVES 4

2 tbsp corn oil
1 tbsp butter
1 leek, sliced thinly
1 large yellow bell pepper, seeded and diced
3 skinless, boneless chicken breasts, diced
1½ cups risotto rice, rinsed
few strands of saffron
6¼ cups hot chicken bouillon
7 oz/200 g canned corn
½ cup toasted unsalted peanuts
½ cup freshly grated Parmesan cheese
salt and pepper

NUTRITION
Calories *701*; Sugars *7 g*; Protein *35 g*; Carbohydrate *88 g*; Fat *26 g*; Saturates *8 g*

   easy

10 mins

30 mins

🍴 **COOK'S TIP**

Risottos can be frozen for up to 1 month, before adding the Parmesan cheese. Remember to reheat the risotto thoroughly as it contains chicken.

The Genoese risotto is cooked in a different way from any of the other risottos. First, you cook the rice, then you prepare a sauce, then you mix the two together. The final result, however, is just as delicious!

Genoese Seafood Risotto

SERVES 4

5 cups hot fish or chicken bouillon
1½ cups risotto rice, rinsed
3 tbsp butter
2 garlic cloves, chopped finely
9 oz/250 g mixed seafood, preferably raw,
    such as shrimp, squid, mussels, and clams
2 tbsp chopped fresh oregano
1¾ oz freshly grated romano or
    Parmesan cheese

1 Place the bouillon in a large pan and bring to a boil over a medium heat. Add the rice and cook for about 12 minutes, stirring, until the rice is tender. Drain thoroughly and set aside any excess liquid.

2 Heat the butter in a large skillet over a low heat. Add the garlic and stir.

3 Add the raw mixed seafood to the skillet and cook for 5 minutes. If the seafood is already cooked, cook for 2–3 minutes.

4 Stir the chopped oregano into the seafood mixture in the skillet.

5 Add the cooked rice to the skillet and cook for 2–3 minutes, stirring, until hot. Add the reserved stock if the mixture gets too sticky. Add the grated cheese and mix well.

6 Transfer the risotto to 4 warmed serving dishes and serve immediately.

NUTRITION
Calories 679; Sugars 1.8 g; Protein 20.7 g;
Carbohydrate 4.7 g; Fat 15.8 g; Saturates 1 g

⭐⭐   easy
🕐   10 mins
🕐   30 mins

 COOK'S TIP

The Genoese are excellent cooks, and they make particularly delicious fish dishes flavored with the local olive oil.

Distinctive-tasting exotic mushrooms, so popular in Italy, give this aromatic risotto a wonderful and robust flavor.

Exotic Mushroom Risotto

1 Place the dried mushrooms in a bowl and pour over enough boiling water to cover. Let soak for 30 minutes, then carefully lift out and pat dry. Strain the soaking liquid through a fine strainer lined with paper towels and set aside.

2 Trim the exotic mushrooms and gently brush clean.

3 Heat 3 tablespoons of the olive oil in a large skillet over a low heat. Add the mixed fresh mushrooms and cook for 1–2 minutes. Add the garlic and the soaked mushrooms and cook, stirring frequently, for 2 minutes. Transfer to a plate and set aside.

4 Heat the remaining olive oil and half the butter in a large pan. Add the onion and cook, stirring occasionally, for about 2 minutes, or until softened. Add the rice and cook, stirring, for about 2 minutes, or until translucent and well coated. Add the vermouth. When almost absorbed, add a ladleful (about 1 cup) of the bouillon. Cook, stirring, until the liquid is absorbed.

5 Continue adding the bouillon, about half a ladleful at a time, letting each addition be completely absorbed before adding the next. This should take 20–25 minutes.

6 Add half the reserved mushroom soaking liquid to the risotto and stir in the mushrooms. Season to taste with salt and pepper and add more mushroom liquid, if necessary. Remove the pan from the heat and stir in the remaining butter, Parmesan cheese, and parsley. Transfer to 6 serving dishes, garnish with parsley sprigs, and serve.

SERVES 6

2 oz/55 g dried porcini or morel mushrooms
about 1 lb 2 oz/500 g mixed fresh exotic mushrooms, such as porcini, girolles, horse mushrooms, and chanterelles, halved if large
4 tbsp olive oil
3–4 garlic cloves, chopped finely
4 tbsp sweet butter
1 onion, chopped finely
3 cups risotto rice, rinsed
¼ cup dry white vermouth
5 cups chicken bouillon, simmering
1⅓ cups freshly grated Parmesan cheese
4 tbsp chopped fresh Italian parsley
salt and pepper

NUTRITION
Calories *425*; Sugars *2 g*; Protein *16 g*;
Carbohydrate *54 g*; Fat *17 g*; Saturates *6 g*

easy

35 mins

35 mins

Try this combination of two types of rice with the richness of pine nuts, basil, and freshly grated Parmesan cheese.

Pesto Rice *with* Garlic Bread

SERVES 4

1½ cups mixed long-grain and wild rice
4 fresh basil sprigs, to garnish
tomato and orange salad, to serve

pesto dressing

15 g/½ oz fresh basil sprigs
1 cup pine nuts
2 garlic cloves, minced
6 tbsp olive oil
¾ cup freshly grated Parmesan cheese
salt and pepper

garlic bread

2 small granary or whole-wheat French
  breadsticks
6 tbsp butter, softened
2 garlic cloves, minced
1 tsp dried mixed herbs

NUTRITION

Calories *918*; Sugars *2 g*; Protein *18 g*;
Carbohydrate *73 g*; Fat *64 g*; Saturates *19 g*

⭐⭐⭐ moderate

🕐 20 mins

🕐 40 mins

1 Place the rice in a pan and cover with water. Bring to a boil over a medium heat and cook for 15–20 minutes. Drain and keep warm.

2 Meanwhile, to make the pesto dressing. Remove the basil leaves from the stalks and finely chop the leaves. Set aside ¼ cup of the pine nuts and finely chop the remainder. Mix with the chopped basil and the remaining dressing ingredients. Alternatively, place all the ingredients in a blender or food processor and blend for a few seconds until smooth. Set aside.

3 To make the garlic bread, slice the bread at 1-inch/2.5-cm intervals, taking care not to slice all the way through. Mix the butter with the garlic and herbs. Season to taste with salt and pepper. Spread thickly between each slice. Wrap the bread in aluminum foil and bake in a preheated oven at 400°F/200°C, for 10–15 minutes.

4 To serve, toast the reserved pine nuts under a preheated medium-hot broiler for 2–3 minutes until golden. Toss the pesto dressing into the hot rice and pile into 4 warmed serving dishes. Sprinkle with toasted pine nuts and garnish with a few basil sprigs. Serve with the garlic bread and a tomato and orange salad.

This traditional Easter risotto pie is from the Piedmont region in northern Italy. Serve it warm or chilled in slices.

Green Easter Pie

1 Lightly grease a 9-inch/23-cm deep cake pan with the butter and line the bottom with baking parchment.

2 Using a sharp knife, coarsely chop the arugula.

3 Heat the olive oil in a skillet over a low heat. Add the onion and garlic and cook for 4–5 minutes, or until softened.

4 Add the rice to the skillet, mix well, then start adding the bouillon a ladleful at a time. Wait until each ladleful of bouillon has been absorbed before adding the next.

5 Cook the mixture, adding the wine, until the rice is tender. This will take at least 20 minutes. Remove the skillet from the heat.

6 Stir in the Parmesan cheese, peas, arugula, tomatoes, eggs, and 2 tablespoons of the marjoram. Season to taste with salt and pepper.

7 Spoon the risotto into the prepared pan and level the surface by pressing down with the back of a wooden spoon. Top with the bread crumbs and remaining marjoram.

8 Bake in a preheated oven at 350°F/ 180°C, for 30 minutes, or until set. Cut into slices and serve immediately.

SERVES 4

1 tbsp butter for greasing
1½ cups arugula
2 tbsp olive oil
1 onion, chopped
2 garlic cloves, chopped
1 cup risotto rice, rinsed
3 cups hot chicken or vegetable bouillon
½ cup white wine
⅔ cup freshly grated Parmesan cheese
1 cup frozen peas, thawed
2 tomatoes, diced
4 eggs, beaten
3 tbsp chopped fresh marjoram
1 cup fresh bread crumbs
salt and pepper

NUTRITION
Calories *392*; Sugars *3 g*; Protein *17 g*;
Carbohydrate *41 g*; Fat *17 g*; Saturates *5 g*

⊛⊛⊛   moderate
🕐   25 mins
🕐   50 mins

Polenta is used in Italy in the same way as potatoes and rice. It has little flavor, but combined with butter, chili, and herbs, it is completely transformed.

Chili Polenta Chips

SERVES 4

6 cups water
2 cups instant polenta
2 tsp chili powder
1 tbsp olive oil or melted butter
⅔ cup sour cream
1 tbsp chopped fresh parsley
salt and pepper

NUTRITION
Calories *365*; Sugars *1 g*; Protein *8 g*;
Carbohydrate *54 g*; Fat *12 g*; Saturates *5 g*

easy

5 mins

20 mins

1 Place the water in a large pan and bring to a boil over a medium heat. Add 2 teaspoons of salt, then add the polenta in a steady stream, stirring.

2 Reduce the heat slightly and continue stirring for about 5 minutes. It is essential to stir the polenta, otherwise it will stick and burn. The polenta should have a thick consistency at this point and should be stiff enough to hold the spoon upright in the pan.

3 Add the chili powder to the polenta mixture and stir well. Season to taste with a little salt and pepper.

4 Spread the polenta out onto a board or cookie sheet to about 1½ inch/4 cm thick. Let cool and set.

5 Cut the cooled polenta mixture into thin wedges.

6 Heat the olive oil in a skillet over a medium heat. Add the polenta wedges and cook for 3–4 minutes on each side, or until golden and crispy. Alternatively, brush with melted butter and broil under a preheated broiler for 6–7 minutes, or until golden. Drain the cooked polenta on paper towels.

7 Mix the sour cream with parsley and place in a bowl.

8 Transfer the polenta to a large serving plate and serve immediately with the sour cream and parsley dip.

Here, skewers of thyme-flavored polenta, wrapped in prosciutto, are broiled or grilled on the barbecue.

Polenta Kabobs *with* Prosciutto

1 Place the water in a large pan and bring to a boil over a medium heat. Add 2 teaspoons of salt, then add the polenta in a steady stream, stirring.

2 Add the fresh thyme leaves to the polenta mixture and season to taste with salt and pepper.

3 Spread out the polenta, about 1 inch/2.5 cm thick, onto a board. Let cool.

4 Using a sharp knife, cut the cooled polenta into 1-inch/2.5-cm cubes.

5 Cut the prosciutto slices into 2 pieces lengthwise. Wrap the prosciutto around the polenta cubes.

6 Thread the wrapped polenta cubes onto presoaked wooden skewers.

7 Brush the kabobs with a little olive oil and cook under a preheated hot broiler, turning frequently, for 7–8 minutes. Alternatively, grill the kabobs over hot coals until golden brown. Transfer to 4 large serving plates and serve with salad greens.

SERVES 4

scant 3¾ cups water
1 cup instant polenta
2 tbsp fresh thyme, stalks removed
8 slices prosciutto, about 2¾ oz/75 g
1 tbsp olive oil
salt and pepper
salad greens, to serve

NUTRITION
Calories *213*; Sugars *27 g*; Protein *34 g*; Carbohydrate *3.2 g*; Fat *7.6 g*; Saturates *4 g*

 easy

5 mins

20 mins

 COOK'S TIP

Try flavoring the polenta with chopped oregano, basil, or marjoram instead of the thyme, if you prefer. You should use 1 tablespoon of chopped herbs to every ⅔ cup instant polenta.

These little potato dumplings are a traditional Italian appetizer but, served with a salad and bread, they make a substantial entrée.

Gnocchi with Herb Sauce

SERVES 6

2 lb /900 g mealy potatoes, cut into
  ½-inch/1-cm pieces
4 tbsp butter
1 egg, beaten
2 cups all-purpose flour
salt and pepper

herb sauce
½ cup olive oil
2 garlic cloves, very finely chopped
1 tbsp chopped fresh oregano
1 tbsp chopped fresh basil
salt and pepper

to serve
freshly grated Parmesan cheese, optional
mixed salad greens
warm ciabatta

NUTRITION
Calories *619*; Sugars *3 g*; Protein *11 g*;
Carbohydrate *81 g*; Fat *30 g*; Saturates *9 g*

 moderate

30 mins

30 mins

1 Bring a large pan of lightly salted water to a boil over a medium heat. Add the potatoes and cook for about 10 minutes, or until tender. Drain.

2 Press the hot potatoes through a strainer into a large bowl. Add 1 teaspoon of salt, the butter, the egg, and 1 cup of the flour. Stir the mixture well to bind together.

3 Turn onto a lightly floured surface and knead, gradually adding the remaining flour, until a smooth, soft, slightly sticky dough is formed.

4 Flour your hands and roll the dough into ¾-inch/2-cm thick rolls. Cut each roll into ¾-inch/2-cm pieces. Press the top of each piece with the floured prongs of a fork and spread out on a lightly floured dish cloth.

5 Bring a large pan of lightly salted water to a gentle simmer over a low heat. Add the gnocchi and cook, in batches, if necessary, for 2–3 minutes, or until they rise to the surface.

6 Remove the gnocchi with a slotted spoon and place in a warmed, greased serving dish. Cover and keep warm.

7 To make the sauce, place the olive oil, garlic, and seasoning in a pan and cook, stirring, for 3–4 minutes until the garlic is golden. Remove from the heat and stir in the herbs. Pour over the gnocchi and serve, sprinkled with Parmesan cheese and accompanied by salad greens and ciabatta.

Try not to handle the mixture too much when making gnocchi, as this will make the dough heavy.

Spinach *and* Ricotta Gnocchi

1 Wash and drain the spinach well and cook in a covered pan without any extra liquid until soft, about 4 minutes. Place the spinach in a strainer and press well to remove as much liquid as possible. Transfer the spinach to a blender and process until smooth. Alternatively, rub through a strainer.

2 Mix the spinach purée with the ricotta, half the romano cheese, the eggs, and nutmeg. Season to taste with salt and pepper, then mix lightly but thoroughly. Work in enough flour, lightly and quickly, to make the mixture easy to handle.

3 Shape the dough quickly into small oval shapes, and dust lightly with flour.

4 Add 1 teaspoon of olive oil to a large pan of lightly salted water and bring to a boil over a medium heat. Add the gnocchi carefully and boil for about 2 minutes, or until they rise to the surface. Using a slotted spoon, transfer the gnocchi to a buttered ovenproof dish. Keep warm.

5 Melt the butter in a skillet over a low heat. Add the pine nuts and raisins and sauté until the nuts start to brown slightly, but do not let the butter burn.

6 Transfer the gnocchi to 4 warmed serving plates, pour the sauce over, and sprinkle with the remaining grated romano cheese. Serve.

SERVES 4

2 lb 4 oz/1 kg spinach
12 oz/350 g ricotta cheese
1½ cups freshly grated romano cheese
3 eggs, beaten
¼ tsp freshly grated nutmeg
all-purpose flour, to mix
1 tsp olive oil
9 tbsp sweet butter, plus extra for greasing
¼ cup pine nuts
½ cup raisins
salt and pepper

NUTRITION
Calories 712; Sugars 15 g; Protein 28 g;
Carbohydrate 16 g; Fat 59 g; Saturates 33 g

⭐⭐⭐ moderate

🕐 20 mins

🕐 15 mins

Semolina has a similar texture to polenta, but is slightly grainier. These gnocchi, which are flavored with cheese and thyme, are easy to make.

Baked Semolina Gnocchi

SERVES 4

1³⁄₄ cups vegetable bouillon
1¹⁄₄ cups semolina
1 tbsp fresh thyme, stalks removed
1 egg, beaten
¹⁄₂ cup freshly grated Parmesan cheese
3¹⁄₂ tbsp butter
2 garlic cloves, minced
salt and pepper

1 Place the vegetable bouillon in a large pan and bring to a boil over a medium heat. Add the semolina in a steady trickle, stirring constantly. Keep stirring for 3–4 minutes, or until the mixture is thick enough to hold a spoon upright. Set aside and let cool slightly.

2 Add the thyme leaves, egg, and half the cheese to the semolina mixture, and season well to taste with salt and pepper.

3 Spread the semolina mixture on to a board to a thickness of ¹⁄₂ inch/12 mm, and let stand until it has cooled and set.

4 When the semolina is cold, cut it into 1-inch/2.5-cm squares and set aside any offcuts.

5 Grease a large ovenproof dish, placing the reserved offcuts in the bottom of the dish. Arrange the semolina squares on top and sprinkle with the remaining cheese.

6 Melt the butter in a pan over a low heat. Add the garlic and season with pepper to taste. Pour the butter mixture over the gnocchi. Bake in a preheated oven, at 425°F/220°C, for 15–20 minutes, or until golden. Serve.

NUTRITION
Calories *259*; Sugars *0 g*; Protein *9 g*;
Carbohydrate *20 g*; Fat *16 g*; Saturates *10 g*

⭐⭐ easy

🕐 15 mins

🕐 30 mins

🍳 COOK'S TIP

Try adding ¹⁄₂ tablespoon of sun-dried tomato paste or ¹⁄₄ cup finely chopped mushrooms, fried in butter, to the semolina mixture in step 2. Follow the same cooking method.

Potatoes are used to make a pasta dough which is cut into thin noodles and boiled. These are served with a creamy bacon and mushroom sauce.

Noodles *with* Cheese Sauce

1 Bring a large pan of water to a boil over a medium heat. Add the potatoes and cook for 10 minutes, or until cooked through. Drain, then mash the potatoes until smooth. Beat in the flour, egg, and milk. Season to taste with salt and pepper and bring together to form a stiff dough.

2 On a lightly floured surface, roll out the dough to form a thin sausage shape. Cut the sausage into 1-inch/2.5-cm lengths. Bring a large pan of lightly salted water to a boil over a medium heat. Drop in the dough pieces and cook for 3–4 minutes. They will rise to the top when cooked.

3 To make the sauce, heat the vegetable oil in a pan over a low heat. Add the onion and garlic and sauté for 2 minutes. Add the mushrooms and bacon and cook for 5 minutes. Stir in the cheese, cream, and parsley. Season to taste with salt and pepper.

4 Drain the noodles and transfer to a warmed serving bowl. Spoon the sauce over the top and toss to mix. Garnish with a parsley sprig and serve.

SERVES 4

1 lb/450 g mealy potatoes, peeled and diced
2 cups all-purpose flour
1 egg, beaten
1 tbsp milk
salt and pepper
1 fresh parsley sprig, to garnish

sauce

1 tbsp vegetable oil
1 onion, chopped
1 garlic clove, minced
4½ oz/125 g open-cap mushrooms, sliced
3 smoked bacon slices, chopped
scant ⅔ cup freshly grated Parmesan cheese
1¼ cups heavy cream
2 tbsp chopped fresh parsley

NUTRITION
Calories *213*; Sugars *1.6 g*; Protein *5 g*;
Carbohydrate *19 g*; Fat *13 g*; Saturates *7 g*

⭐⭐ easy
🥄 5 mins
🕐 20 mins

 COOK'S TIP

Make the dough in advance, then wrap and store the noodles in the refrigerator for up to 24 hours.

Desserts

For many people the favorite part of any meal is the dessert. The recipes that have been selected here will be a treat for all palates. Whether you are a chocolate lover or on a diet, in this chapter there is a recipe to tempt you. Choose from a light summer delicacy or a hearty hot winter treat—you will find desserts to indulge in all year round. If you are looking for a chilled sweet, choose the rich Vanilla Ice Cream, or if a warm dessert takes your fancy, Crispy-Topped Fruit Bake will do the trick.

This melt-in-your-mouth version of a favorite cake has a fraction of the fat of the traditional version.

Carrot *and* Ginger Cake

SERVES 10

1 tbsp butter for greasing
1¾ cups all-purpose flour
1 tsp baking powder
1 tsp baking soda
2 tsp ground ginger
½ tsp salt
¾ cup molasses sugar
1⅔ cups grated carrots
2 pieces chopped preserved ginger
1 tbsp grated fresh gingerroot
generous ⅓ cup seedless raisins
2 eggs, beaten
3 tbsp corn oil
juice of 1 orange

frosting
1 cup lowfat soft cheese
4 tbsp confectioners' sugar
1 tsp vanilla extract

to decorate
carrot, grated
preserved ginger, grated
ground ginger

NUTRITION
Calories *249*; Sugars *28 g*; Protein *7 g*;
Carbohydrate *46 g*; Fat *6 g*; Saturates *1 g*

⭐⭐⭐   moderate

🕐   15 mins

🕐   1 hr 15 mins

1 Grease and line an 8-inch/20-cm round cake pan with baking parchment.

2 Sift the flour, baking powder, baking soda, ground ginger, and salt into a bowl. Stir in the sugar, carrots, preserved ginger, gingerroot, and raisins. Beat the eggs, oil, and orange juice together, then pour into the bowl. Mix the ingredients together well.

3 Spoon the mixture into the prepared pan and bake in the preheated oven at 350°F/180°C, for 1–1¼ hours, or until firm to the touch and a toothpick inserted into the center of the cake comes out clean. Let cool in the pan.

4 To make the frosting, place the soft cheese in a bowl and, using a wooden spoon, beat to soften. Sift in the confectioners' sugar and add the vanilla extract. Mix well.

5 Remove the cake from the pan and smooth the frosting over the top. Decorate with grated carrot, grated ginger, and ground ginger. Serve.

The sugar lumps give a lovely crunchy topping to this easy blackberry and apple dessert.

Crispy-Topped Fruit Bake

1 Grease and line a 2-lb/900-g loaf pan with baking parchment. Place the cooking apples in a pan with the lemon juice, then bring to a boil over a medium heat. Reduce the heat, cover, and let simmer for about 10 minutes, or until softened and pulpy. Beat well and let cool.

2 Strain the flour, baking powder, and cinnamon into a bowl, adding any husks that remain in the strainer. Stir in ½ cup of the blackberries and the sugar.

3 Make a well in the center of the ingredients and add the egg, yogurt, and cooled apple purée. Mix well to incorporate thoroughly. Spoon the mixture into the prepared loaf pan and level the top.

4 Sprinkle with the remaining blackberries, pressing them down into the cake mixture, and top with the crushed sugar lumps. Bake in a preheated oven at 375°F/190°C, for 40–45 minutes. Remove the cake from the oven and let cool in the pan.

5 Remove the cooled cake from the pan and peel away the baking parchment. Dust with cinnamon and decorate with extra blackberries and apple slices, then serve.

🎩 **COOK'S TIP**

Try replacing the blackberries with blueberries. Use the canned or frozen variety if fresh blueberries are unavailable.

SERVES 4

1 tbsp butter for greasing
12 oz/350 g tart cooking apples, peeled, cored, and diced
3 tbsp lemon juice
2½ cups self-rising whole-wheat flour
½ tsp baking powder
1 tsp ground cinnamon, plus extra for dusting
¾ cup blackberries, thawed if frozen, plus extra to decorate
¾ cup molasses sugar
1 egg, beaten
scant 1 cup lowfat plain yogurt
2 oz/55 g white or brown sugar lumps, crushed lightly
1 dessert apple, sliced, to decorate

NUTRITION
Calories 227; Sugars 30 g; Protein 5 g;
Carbohydrate 53 g; Fat 1 g; Saturates 0.2 g

⭐⭐⭐   moderate
     15 mins
     55 mins

A substantial cake that is ideal served with coffee. The mashed bananas help to keep the cake moist, and the lime frosting gives it extra zest.

Banana *and* Lime Cake

SERVES 10

1 tbsp butter for greasing
generous 2 cups all-purpose flour
1 tsp salt
1½ tsp baking powder
scant 1 cup light brown sugar
1 tsp grated lime peel
1 egg, beaten lightly
1 banana, mashed with 1 tbsp lime juice
⅔ cup lowfat plain yogurt
⅔ cup golden raisins

topping
generous 1 cup confectioners' sugar
1–2 tsp lime juice
½ tsp finely grated lime peel

to decorate
banana chips
finely grated lime peel

NUTRITION
Calories *235*; Sugars *31 g*; Protein *5 g*;
Carbohydrate *55 g*; Fat *1 g*; Saturates *0.3 g*

⭐⭐   easy

🕐   35 mins

🕐   45 mins

1 Grease and line a large, deep 7-inch/18-cm round cake pan with baking parchment.

2 Sift the flour, salt, and baking powder into a large mixing bowl and stir in the sugar and lime peel.

3 Make a well in the center of the dry ingredients and add the egg, banana, yogurt, and golden raisins. Mix well until thoroughly incorporated.

4 Spoon the mixture into the prepared pan and level the surface. Bake in a preheated oven at 350°F/180°C, for 40–45 minutes, or until firm to the touch and a toothpick inserted into the center comes out clean. Let cool in the pan for 10 minutes, then turn out onto a wire rack to cool completely.

5 To make the topping, strain the confectioners' sugar into a small bowl and mix with the lime juice to form a soft, but not too runny, frosting. Stir in the lime peel. Drizzle the lime frosting over the top of the cake, letting it run down the sides.

6 Decorate the cake with banana chips and lime peel. Before serving, let the cake stand for 15 minutes to let the frosting set.

These have a slightly different texture from traditional biscuits, but they are just as delicious served warm and spread with butter.

Potato *and* Nutmeg Cookies

1 Grease and line a cookie sheet with baking parchment. Bring a large pan of water to a boil over a medium heat. Add the diced potatoes and cook for 10 minutes, or until softened.

2 Drain and mash the potatoes, transfer to a large mixing bowl, and stir in the flour, baking powder, and nutmeg. Stir in the golden raisins, egg, and cream, and beat with a spoon until smooth.

3 Shape the mixture into 8 rounds, ¾ inch/2 cm thick, and place on the prepared cookie sheet.

4 Cook in a preheated oven at 400°F/200°C, for about 15 minutes, or until the biscuits have risen and are golden. Sprinkle the biscuits with the sugar and serve warm, spread with butter, if you wish.

SERVES 4

1 tbsp butter for greasing
1⅓ cups diced mealy potatoes
⅓ cup all-purpose flour
1½ tsp baking powder
½ tsp grated nutmeg
⅓ cup golden raisins
1 egg, beaten
3 tbsp heavy cream
2 tsp soft light brown sugar

NUTRITION
Calories 135; Sugars 6 g; Protein 3 g;
Carbohydrate 23 g; Fat 4 g; Saturates 2 g

⭐⭐ easy
🕐 5 mins
🕐 25 mins

 COOK'S TIP

For extra convenience, make a batch of biscuits in advance and open-freeze them. Thaw thoroughly and warm in a preheated medium-hot oven when ready to serve.

Known as zabaglione in Italy, this warm mousse will not keep, so make it fresh and serve immediately in tall glasses.

Egg Mousse *with* Marsala

SERVES 4

5 egg yolks
½ cup superfine sugar
⅔ cup Marsala wine or sweet sherry
amaretti cookies, to serve (optional)

1 Place the egg yolks in a mixing bowl. Add the sugar and whisk until the mixture is thick and very pale and has doubled in volume.

2 Place the bowl containing the whisked egg yolks and sugar mixture over a pan of simmering water.

3 Add the Marsala wine or sherry to the egg yolk and sugar mixture and continue whisking until the foam mixture becomes warm. This process may take as long as 10 minutes.

4 Pour the mixture, which should be foamy and light, into 4 tall wine glasses.

5 Serve the mousse warm with fresh fruit or amaretti cookies, if you wish.

NUTRITION
Calories *158*; Sugars *29 g*; Protein *1 g*;
Carbohydrate *29 g*; Fat *1 g*; Saturates *0.2 g*

COOK'S TIP

Any other type of liqueur may be used instead of the Marsala wine or sweet sherry, if you prefer. Serve soft fruits, such as strawberries or raspberries, with the mousse—it's a delicious combination!

easy

15 mins

10 mins

As this recipe uses only a little chocolate, choose one with a minimum of 70 per cent cocoa solids for a good flavor.

Chocolate Egg Mousse

1 Place the egg yolks and superfine sugar together in a large glass bowl and, using an electric whisk, whisk until the mixture is very pale.

2 Grate the chocolate finely and fold into the egg mixture.

3 Fold the Marsala wine into the chocolate mixture.

4 Place the mixing bowl over a pan of gently simmering water and set the electric whisk on the lowest speed or change to a hand-held balloon whisk. Cook gently, whisking until the mixture thickens. Take care not to overcook or the mixture will curdle.

5 Spoon the hot mixture into warmed individual glass dishes or coffee cups and serve as soon as possible so it is warm, light, and fluffy, accompanied by amaretti cookies.

SERVES 4

4 egg yolks
4 tbsp superfine sugar
1¾ oz/50 g dark chocolate
½ cup Marsala wine
amaretti cookies, to serve

NUTRITION
Calories 227; Sugars 29 g; Protein 19 g;
Carbohydrate 29 g; Fat 9.3 g; Saturates 0.4 g

⭐⭐ easy

🕐 10 mins

🕐 5 mins

 COOK'S TIP

Make the dessert just before serving as it will separate if you let it stand. If it starts to curdle, remove from the heat immediately and place in a bowl of cold water to stop the cooking. Whisk furiously until the mixture comes together.

This quick version of one of the most popular Italian desserts is ready in a matter of minutes.

Quick Tiramisù

SERVES 4

1 cup mascarpone or full-fat soft cheese
1 egg, separated
2 tbsp plain yogurt
2 tbsp superfine sugar
2 tbsp dark rum
2 tbsp strong black coffee
8 lady-fingers
2 tbsp grated dark chocolate

1 Place the cheese in a large bowl, add the egg yolk and yogurt, and, using a wooden spoon, beat until smooth.

2 Using a whisk, whisk the egg white in a separate, spotlessly clean, greasefree bowl until stiff but not dry, then whisk in the sugar and carefully fold into the cheese mixture.

3 Spoon half of the mixture into 4 tall glasses.

4 Mix the rum and coffee together in a shallow dish. Dip the lady-fingers into the rum mixture, break them in half, or into smaller pieces if necessary, and divide among the glasses.

5 Stir any of the remaining rum and coffee mixture into the remaining cheese and spoon over the top.

6 Sprinkle with grated chocolate and serve immediately. Alternatively, chill in the refrigerator until required.

NUTRITION
Calories 387; Sugars 17 g; Protein 9 g;
Carbohydrate 22 g; Fat 28 g; Saturates 15 g

⭐⭐⭐   moderate
🕑   15 mins
🕐   0 mins

👨‍🍳 **COOK'S TIP**

Mascarpone is an Italian soft cream cheese made from cow's milk. It has a rich, silky smooth texture, and a deliciously creamy flavor. It can be eaten as it is with fresh fruits or flavored with coffee or chocolate.

This is the ultimate in self-indulgence—a truly delicious dessert that tastes every bit as good as it looks.

Raspberry Almond Spirals

1 Bring a large pan of lightly salted water to a boil over a medium heat. Add the pasta and cook until just done. Drain thoroughly, then return to the pan and let cool.

2 Using the back of a spoon, firmly press ⅓ cup of the raspberries through a strainer set over a large mixing bowl to form a smooth purée.

3 Put the raspberry purée and sugar in a small pan and let simmer over low heat, stirring occasionally, for 5 minutes. Stir in the lemon juice and set the sauce aside until required.

4 Add the remaining raspberries to the pasta in the pan and mix together well. Transfer the raspberry and pasta mixture to a serving dish.

5 Spread the almonds out on a cookie sheet and toast under a preheated hot broiler until golden brown. Remove and let cool slightly.

6 Stir the raspberry liqueur into the reserved raspberry sauce and mix together until very smooth. Pour the raspberry sauce over the pasta, then generously sprinkle over the toasted almonds, and serve.

SERVES 4

½ cup fusilli
4 cups raspberries
2 tbsp superfine sugar
1 tbsp lemon juice
4 tbsp slivered almonds
3 tbsp raspberry liqueur

NUTRITION
Calories 235; Sugars 20 g; Protein 7 g; Carbohydrate 36 g; Fat 7 g; Saturates 1 g

⭐⭐ easy
5 mins
20 mins

 COOK'S TIP

You could use almost any sweet, really ripe berry for making this dessert. Strawberries and blackberries are especially suitable, combined with the correspondingly flavored liqueur.

If you prepare these in advance, all you have to do is pop the peaches on the barbecue grill when you are ready to serve them.

Peaches *with* Mascarpone

SERVES 4

4 firm but ripe fresh peaches
¾ cup mascarpone cheese
⅓ cup pecan nuts or walnuts, chopped
1 tsp corn oil
4 tbsp maple syrup

1 Cut the peaches in half and remove the pits. If you are preparing this recipe in advance, press the peach halves together again and wrap them in plastic wrap until required.

2 Combine the mascarpone cheese and pecan nuts or walnuts in a small bowl. Let chill in the refrigerator until required.

3 When ready to serve, brush the peaches with a little corn oil and place on a grill rack set over medium hot coals. Cook the peaches for 5–10 minutes, turning once, until hot.

4 Transfer the peaches to a serving dish and top with the mascarpone cheese and nut mixture. Drizzle the maple syrup over the peaches and mascarpone cheese filling and serve immediately.

NUTRITION
Calories *301*; Sugars *24 g*; Protein *6 g*;
Carbohydrate *24 g*; Fat *20 g*; Saturates *9 g*

 very easy

 10 mins

🕐 10 mins

👨‍🍳 **COOK'S TIP**

You can use nectarines instead of peaches for this recipe. Remember to choose ripe, but firm, fruit which won't go soft and mushy when it is grilled. Prepare the nectarines in the same way as the peaches and grill for 5–10 minutes.

Italy is synonymous with ice cream. This homemade version of real Italian vanilla ice cream is absolutely delicious and so easy to make.

Vanilla Ice Cream

1 Place the cream in a heavy-bottomed pan and heat over a low heat, whisking constantly. Add the vanilla bean, lemon peel, eggs, and egg yolks and heat until the mixture reaches just below boiling point.

2 Reduce the heat and cook for about 8–10 minutes, whisking the mixture constantly, until thickened. Stir the sugar into the cream mixture, set aside and let cool, then strain the cream mixture through a strainer.

3 Slit open the vanilla bean, scoop out the seeds, and stir into the cream.

4 Pour the mixture into a shallow freezing container and freeze for 1 hour, then remove from the freezer and beat to break up the ice crystals. Return to the freezer and continue freezing. Repeat beating and freezing several times. Cover with a lid and store in the freezer until required. Transfer to the refrigerator just before serving to soften slightly.

SERVES 4

2½ cups heavy cream
1 vanilla bean
pared peel of 1 lemon
4 eggs, beaten
2 egg yolks
¾ cup superfine sugar

NUTRITION

Calories *652*; Sugars *33 g*; Protein *8 g*; Carbohydrate *33 g*; Fat *55 g*; Saturates *32 g*

   easy

5 mins

10 mins

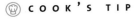 **COOK'S TIP**

Ice cream is one of the traditional dishes of Italy. Everyone eats it and there are numerous *gelato* stalls selling a wide variety of flavors, usually in a cone.

These luxury cookies will be popular at any time of the year, but they make a particularly wonderful treat at Christmas.

Florentines

MAKES 10

4 tbsp butter
¼ cup superfine sugar
scant ¼ cup all-purpose flour, strained
⅓ cup almonds, chopped
⅓ cup chopped candied peel
¼ cup raisins, chopped
2 tbsp chopped candied cherries
finely grated peel of ½ lemon
4½ oz/125 g unsweetened chocolate, melted

1 Line 2 large cookie sheets with baking parchment.

2 Heat the butter and sugar in a small pan over a low heat until the butter has just melted and the sugar dissolved. Remove the pan from the heat.

3 Stir in the flour and mix well. Stir in the chopped almonds, mixed peel, raisins, cherries, and lemon peel. Place teaspoonfuls of the mixture well apart on the cookie sheets. Bake in a preheated oven at 350°F/180°C, for about 10 minutes, or until lightly golden.

4 As soon as the florentines are removed from the oven, press the edges into neat shapes while still on the cookie sheets with a cookie cutter. Let cool on the cookie sheets until firm, then transfer to a wire rack to cool completely.

5 Spread the melted chocolate over the smooth side of each florentine. As the chocolate begins to set, mark wavy lines in it with a fork. Let the florentines set, chocolate side up.

NUTRITION
Calories *164*; Sugars *20 g*; Protein *2.5 g*;
Carbohydrate *12.8 g*; Fat *10 g*; Saturates *7.5 g*

    easy

50 mins

10 mins

 COOK'S TIP

Replace the unsweetened chocolate with white chocolate or cover half of the florentines in unsweetened chocolate and half in white.

A wonderful mixture of summer fruits encased in slices of white bread which soak up all the deep red, flavorful juices.

Summer Puddings

1 Grease six ²/₃-cup molds with a little butter or oil.

2 Line the molds with the bread, cutting the slices to fit snugly.

3 Place the sugar in a small pan with the water and heat gently over a low heat, stirring frequently until dissolved, then bring to a boil over a high heat and boil for 2 minutes.

4 Set aside 6 large strawberries for decoration. Add half the raspberries and the rest of the fruits to the syrup, cutting the strawberries in half if large, and let simmer gently for a few minutes, until they are starting to soften but still retain their shape.

5 Spoon the fruits and some of the liquid into the molds. Cover with more slices of bread. Spoon a little juice around the sides of the molds so the bread is well soaked. Cover with a saucer and a heavy weight, let cool, then chill thoroughly in the refrigerator, preferably overnight.

6 Process the remaining raspberries in a blender or food processor, or press through a non-metallic strainer. Add a little extra liquid to the raspberries if necessary to give the sauce a coating consistency.

7 Turn onto 4 serving plates and spoon the raspberry sauce over. Decorate with the mint sprigs and reserved strawberries, and serve with cream.

SERVES 6

1 tbsp vegetable oil or butter for greasing
6–8 thin slices white bread, crusts removed
¾ cup superfine sugar
1¼ cups water
½ lb/225 g strawberries
1 lb/450 g raspberries
1¼ cups blackcurrants and/or redcurrants
1½ cups blackberries or loganberries
4 fresh mint sprigs, to decorate
pouring cream, to serve

NUTRITION
Calories 250; Sugars 41 g; Protein 4 g; Carbohydrate 53 g; Fat 4 g; Saturates 2 g

 moderate

 10 mins

10 mins

This famous Tuscan honey and nut cake is a Christmas speciality. In Italy it is sold in pretty boxes, and served in very thin slices.

Panforte *di* Siena

SERVES 4

1 cup almonds, halved
1 cup hazelnuts
1/2 cup chopped mixed peel
1 cup no-soak dried apricots
1/2 cup glacé or crystallized pineapple
grated peel of 1 large orange
1/2 cup plain flour
2 tbsp unsweetened cocoa
2 tsp ground cinnamon
1/2 cup superfine sugar
1/2 cup honey
confectioners' sugar, for dredging

NUTRITION

Calories *257*; Sugars *29 g*; Protein *5 g*;
Carbohydrate *33 g*; Fat *13 g*; Saturates *1 g*

  moderate

🍳 10 mins

🕐 1 hr 15 mins

1 Place the almonds onto a large cookie sheet and toast under a preheated hot broiler until lightly browned. Place in a bowl.

2 Place the hazelnuts onto a large cookie sheet and toast under the preheated hot broiler until the skins split. Place on a dry tea towel and rub off the skins. Coarsely chop the hazelnuts and add them to the almonds along with the mixed peel.

3 Chop the apricots and pineapple finely, add to the nuts with the orange peel and mix well.

4 Strain the flour with the cocoa and cinnamon, add to the nut mixture and mix.

5 Line a round 8-inch/20-cm cake pan or deep loose-bottomed flan pan with baking parchment.

6 Place the sugar and honey in a pan and heat over a low heat until the sugar dissolves. Increase the heat and boil gently for about 5 minutes, or until the mixture thickens and starts to turn a deeper shade of brown. Quickly add to the nut mixture and stir well to mix evenly. Turn into the prepared pan and level the top using the back of a damp spoon.

7 Bake the cake in a preheated oven at 300°F/150°C, for 1 hour. Remove from the oven and let cool in the pan until completely cold. Take out of the pan and carefully peel off the paper parchment. Before serving, dredge the cake heavily with strained confectioners' sugar and serve in very thin slices.

This cheesecake takes a little time to prepare and cook, but is well worth the effort. It is quite rich and is good served with some fresh fruit, such as cape gooseberries.

Chocolate Cheesecake

1 Place the flour, ground almonds, and 1 tablespoon of the sugar in a bowl and mix well. Rub the margarine into the mixture to form a dough.

2 Lightly grease and line the bottom of a 9-inch/23-cm springform pan with baking parchment. Press the dough into the bottom of the pan, pushing the dough right up to the edge of the pan.

3 Coarsely chop the bean curd and place in a food processor with the vegetable oil, orange juice, brandy, unsweetened cocoa, almond extract, and remaining sugar and process until smooth and creamy. Pour over the base in the pan and cook in a preheated oven at 325°F/160°C, for about 1–1¼ hours, or until set.

4 Let cool in the pan for 5 minutes, then remove from the pan and chill in the refrigerator. Dust with confectioners' sugar and unsweetened cocoa. Decorate with cape gooseberries and serve.

SERVES 12

generous ¾ cup all-purpose flour
scant 1 cup ground almonds
scant 1 cup molasses sugar
scant ¾ cup margarine
1½ lb/675 g firm bean curd (drained weight)
¾ cup vegetable oil
½ cup orange juice
¾ cup brandy
6 tbsp unsweetened cocoa, plus extra to decorate
2 tsp almond extract

to decorate
confectioners' sugar
cape gooseberries (golden berries)

NUTRITION
Calories *471*; Sugars *20 g*; Protein *10 g*;
Carbohydrate *28 g*; Fat *33 g*; Saturates *5 g*

moderate

1 hr 15 mins

1 hr 15 mins

🍳 **COOK'S TIP**

Cape gooseberries make an attractive decoration for many desserts. Peel open the papery husks to expose the bright orange fruits.

Index